SOUTHERN ESSEX

Edited by Donna Samworth

First published in Great Britain in 2003 by
YOUNG WRITERS
Remus House,
Coltsfoot Drive,
Peterborough, PE2 9JX
Telephone (01733) 890066

HB ISBN 0 75434 297 2
SB ISBN 0 75434 298 0

FOREWORD

This year, the Young Writers' The Write Stuff! competition proudly presents a showcase of the best poetic talent from over 40,000 up-and-coming writers nationwide.

Young Writers was established in 1991 and we are still successful, even in today's modern world, in promoting and encouraging the reading and writing of poetry.

The thought, effort, imagination and hard work put into each poem impressed us all, and once again, the task of selecting poems was a difficult one, but nevertheless, an enjoyable experience.

We hope you are as pleased as we are with the final selection and that you and your family continue to be entertained with *The Write Stuff! Southern Essex* for many years to come.

CONTENTS

Braeside Senior School

Leena Patel	1
Olamide Kupoluyi	1
Jerry Huzzey	1
Jasmin Valera	2
Nicola Lowe	2
Clare McDonald	2
Margaux Botha	3
Sian Ager	3
Sachleen Chana	4
Hannah Cochran	4
Zoë Pounder	4
Ysanne Harding	5
Catherine Waithe-Arnold	5
Leanne Frost	5
Katerina Pastov	6
Sophie Wise	6
Sarah Robertson	6
Emma Mansfield	6
Stephanie Hillman	7
Maansi Valera	7
Catherine Thomas	7
Louise Robertson	7

Cecil Jones High School

Scott Cole	8
Steven Lang	8
Daniel Compton	9
Hannah Axcell	10
Graham Fuller	10
Samantha Boxall	11
Samantha Saunders	12
Thomas Jarvis	12
Terry Millington	13
Krystine Gallagher	14
Jade Morris	14

Jessica Boxall	15
Hayley Watts	16
Leanne Hodgson	16
Peter Martin	17
Jenny Metcalfe	17
Adam Thorogood	18

Chafford Hundred Campus

Holly Fordham	18
Matthew Tansley	19
Natasha Lane	20
Charles Dack	20
James Johnson	21
Connor Grover	22
Riya Bernard	22
Andrew Woollard	23
Claire Dale	24
Aaron Smith	25
Scott Hyland	26
Andrew Dark	26
Brogan Connolly	27
Amy Blundell	28
Charlie Court	28
Joseph Leonardi	29
Hollie Willmot	29
Abbi Reid	30
Colin Moy	30
Shaan Patel	31
Celen Hurbas	32
Kymberley Jamieson	32
Abigail Hawkins	33
Charlotte Cullen	34
Aaron Merrigan	34
Frankie Howe	35
Ashley Watson	35
Jeffrey Huynh	36
Robyn Freeman	36
Jamie Hanks	37

	Steven Blake	38
	Emily Higgs	39
	Roseanne Howard	40
	Jasmin Skeet	40
Cranbrook College		
	Ranvir Singh Bhogal	41
	Marcus Dyal	41
	Alex Deakin	42
	Sagar Desai	43
	Benoy Soman	44
	Timothy Lee	44
	Michael Khoshdel	45
	Naseer Hayath	46
	Zubair Altaf	47
	Ian Gregory	48
	Nilesh Bodalia	48
	Farhaan Akoo	49
	Ashfaaq Patel	50
	Gurnam Chagar	50
	Carl Anka	51
	Mohammed Kothia	52
	Amarjeet Singh Sohal	52
	Saliya Jayaweera	53
	Matthew Patterson-Muir	54
	Rahul Ravalia	54
	Sukhdeep Sangha	55
	Arvind Nair	56
	Rizwan Syed	56
	Piyush Patel	57
	Sunjay Bhudia	58
	Nikesh Patel	58
	Kishen Nakum	59
	Quikobad Hussain	59
	Debo Adebayo	60
	Asfan Sheikh	61
	Rinu Senan	62
	Absher Mansoor	62

	Indveer Kataria	63
	Isuru Perera	64
	Davender Shergill	64
	Rajen Raniga	65
	Irfaan Karim	66
	Tauseef Amjad	66
	Dhruv Patel	67
	Jayson Mcleod	68
	Jerome Heron	68
	Jack Allman	69
	Joshua Wariebi	70
	Michael Myint	70
	Sahal Quazi	71
	Ajay Bhaskaran	71
	Luchien Anderson	72
	Ibrahim Ahmed	72
	Tisaru Perera	73
	Asim Bhuta	74
	Jaimin Patel	75
Havering Sixth Form College		
	Simon Brindley	76
Sanders Draper School		
	Robert Clark	77
	Sebastian Massart	77
	Rebecca Warren	78
	Ameer Nasir	78
	Reema Chandni Unnadkat	79
	Jack Bruce	79
	Stephanie Driscoll	80
	Michael Chaplin	80
	Natalie Spilsbury	81
	Elizabeth Boyle	81
	Jennifer Phelan	82
	Samantha Holt	82
	William Morris	83
	Charlotte Russell	84

Daniel Jones	85
Melissa Knight	85
Lenita Rankin	86
Jade Allen	86
Stephanie Randleson	87
Laura Dennis	88
Sasha Tyler	89
Charlotte Watts	89
Thomas Pockett	90
Michaela Wilson	90
Danielle Young	90
James Melrose	91
Michael Titmus	91
Chukuma (Chuck) Pratt	92
Dean Williams	92
Simon Weinand	93
Katy Stallan	93
Frank Rex	94
Daniel O'Neill	94
Jack Wilkinson	95
Chelsea Richardson	95
Lewis Harrison	96
Paul Kelley	96
Nikki Eves	97
Callum Pearman	97
Daniel Ridley	98
Samantha Barnes	98
Zachary Chouman	99
Nicky Wells	99
Matthew Haywood	100
Maria Dunn	100
Josh Oakley	101
Sam O'Vens	101
Scott Tungatt	102
Marianna Alexandrou	102
Chantelle Carter	103
Grace Sussex	104
Ashley Benningfield	104

Toni Watson	105
Amy Munro	106
Alicia Thompson	106
Jody Overington	107
Victoria Coleman	107
Jade Clark	108
Jake McGuinness	108
Rebecca Holman	109
Rio Caley	109
Kelsey Oates	110
Laura Pickess	110
Emma Matthews	111
Elisabeth Mann	111
Nadene Kennedy	112
Jamie Taylor	112
Anneka Fisher	113
Sarah Connor	113
Amie O'Keefe	114
Calum Sharp	114
Lauran Lechmere	115

William Edwards School

Rhys Battye	115
Thomas Gilbank	116
John Thompson	116
Daniel Gray	117
Joe Pavitt	118
Laura Sach	118
Kelly Broadbent	119
Jacob Smith	119
Colin Oakley	120
Thomas Wyborn	120
Adam Walters	121
Simeran Ghataora	121
Charlotte Hinton	122
James Bell	122
Hayley Pulfer	123
Jade Barker	123

Sarah Mitchell	124
Brooke Mason	124
Frank Attah	125
Crystal Gansbuhler	125
Lauren Devereaux	126
Alexandrea Palmer	126
Christopher Webb	127
Antony Lane	127
Alex Douglas	128
Lesley Biggins	128
Craig Siddons	129
Phillip Whelpton	129
Ben Kelly	130
Ellis Goldsmith	130
Andrew Baker	131
Rebecca Gray	131
Dilvinder Sander	132
Billy Harvey	132
Seema Malvankar	133
Lee Buttner	133
Aaron Riley	134
Chevelle Harwood	134
Jenna Yeomans	135
Elizabeth Colledge	135
Chris Beven	136
Louis Hawker	136
Adam Rixson	137
Katie West	138
William Plom	139

The Poems

SPACE

Floating high above the rest
Makes you feel like the best,
Free from all your troubles below,
Makes you feel good and glow.
The stars up high are twinkling,
They look as if they are winking.
The moon fills the sky like
A piece of pie.

I love space.

Leena Patel (13)
Braeside Senior School

THE APPLE

Apples are my favourite fruit
to eat.
The juice inside makes them
so sweet.

Olamide Kupoluyi (13)
Braeside Senior School

MY DOG

A polka dot dress lying on the floor
as greedy as a pig
as gentle as a butterfly.

Jerry Huzzey (13)
Braeside Senior School

SKIING

Sliding swiftly,
Down the steep, snowy mountain,
Faster and faster,
Through the curves and bends,
No way else but down,
Past the glistening trees,
Wind rushing in my face,
It feels ace.

Jasmin Valera (13)
Braeside Senior School

TUNNELS OF STONE

A green audience of grass,
A spider-webbed tree,
Underneath and above the tunnels of stone.

Nicola Lowe (12)
Braeside Senior School

THE GARDEN QUEUE

Grass in front of a bench,
Spreads as far as the eye can see,
Like some green hedgehogs waiting to go into a tunnel.

Clare McDonald (13)
Braeside Senior School

My Poem

I'm opening my book,
Flicking through the pages
Having a look!

I'm now picking up my pen
Not thinking of men
We're talking to Mrs Dongworth
Explaining what we are doing
Whilst everyone else is booing!

We are going to our desks
Thinking of an idea
Which is really an annoying pest.

That's it, Finished.
No more poem left,
But I know it
Will be the best.

Margaux Botha
Braeside Senior School

Bestest Mates

Daisy and Emma are always together,
they're always up for a laugh.
Then there are Bal and Zara too.
They are always mucking about.
That leaves us Jess and Sian,
we're bestest mates
for ever and ever.

Sian Ager (14)
Braeside Senior School

RAINY DAYS

I hate rainy days,
it's boring, boring.
The clouds keep on
pouring, pouring.
I can hear the thunder
roaring, roaring.

Sachleen Chana (13)
Braeside Senior School

FREEDOM

Swimming through the cool blue water,
A feel of freedom as you go,
Diving down, swimming up,
Whirling round, out of reach,
Water swirling through fingers and toes.

Hannah Cochran (13)
Braeside Senior School

JUNGLE IN MY GARDEN

The blades of grass are like green liquorice,
The twigs of the trees look like spiders' webs,
The flowers dance around the fir tree.

Zoë Pounder (12)
Braeside Senior School

Billy

It was a normal day
And it started out okay,
Dad said they were going to have another one,
It was going to be my mum's first son.

The day came on October 7th,
It was 4 o'clock in the morning.
Mum and Dad woke me up
And I couldn't stop yawning.

The baby came. He was so cute,
He was really tiny and sweet,
We named him Billy. It suited him
And he has changed my life since.

Ysanne Harding (13)
Braeside Senior School

The Garden Through The Window

The trees' bare branches are like a labyrinth of sticks
You can hear the serenade of the invisible birds
And hear the whispers of the stone benches, the immortal storytellers.

Catherine Waithe-Arnold (12)
Braeside Senior School

Flower Audience

The spring flowers bright and colourful,
Circle the tall fir tree,
Like an audience watching.

Leanne Frost (12)
Braeside Senior School

The Wild Jungle

The flowers are like plums and grapes,
The trees remind me of a film jungle,
The grass is like a still green sea.

Katerina Pastov (12)
Braeside Senior School

My Mini Jungle

The bush in the garden with the cauliflower tops,
The blades of apple liquorice grass,
All remind me of a mini jungle where everything stares at me!

Sophie Wise (12)
Braeside Senior School

The Secret Garden

Pigeons like fat men,
Plodding through the tunnel benches,
under the bare trees, like bald men.

Sarah Robertson (12)
Braeside Senior School

Unusual Gardens

Pale yellow-green bush like a jelly monster,
Yellow elves playing their golden trumpets,
The big, fat pigeons perched on the wall like rich businessmen.

Emma Mansfield (13)
Braeside Senior School

Green And Pink Poem

Blossom trees stand up tall,
I give a branch a little pull,
then onto the green, green grass,
the pink candyfloss falls.

Stephanie Hillman (12)
Braeside Senior School

Spring Flowers Around A Tree

Dancing around the musical tree
Yellow elves playing trumpets
On a still stained sea.

Maansi Valera (12)
Braeside Senior School

The Green Garden

The fir tree looks like a green giant monster,
grass like green sea.
The flowers under the tree look like an audience.

Catherine Thomas (12)
Braeside Senior School

The Wild Jungle

Grass blades like liquorice sticks,
Flowers watching people play,
Stone benches like tunnels in a playground.

Louise Robertson (12)
Braeside Senior School

CITY OF FEAR

As night draws in, the light-hearted hooligans approach,
Calm is whipped by the roar of engines,
Joyriders come into power and abolish law,
The noise is ear-splitting, unbearable.

Newspapers echo horrible, unthinkable news:
People's lives torn apart from flesh to bone.
The blood thickens,
More red liquid of death to be spilled -
Waiting for the next murder.

Groups stand around in death defying gangs,
Their need for self harm gets the better of them.
Fear catches you,
What could happen next?
They swallow poisons like Smarties . . . more and more.

As I walk around this place of rejection and punishment,
Traffic anxiously forces its way through the down and out streets;
A death-causing accident waiting to happen.

Scott Cole (14)
Cecil Jones High School

PROUD TO BE ENGLISH

The patriotic English crowd,
Who wave their flags and sing aloud,
An Englishman till death they vow,
A part of which I am so proud.

The envy that it generates,
To foreigners from alien states,
Who pack their bags and flood our gates.
Our freedom to participate.

Through centuries of ups and downs,
We've still retained the English Crown,
Our sovereign lives in London Town,
So regal in her ermine gown.

For England is my champion,
History shows what we have done,
Battles fought and battles won,
The pioneers of three lions.

Steven Lang (15)
Cecil Jones High School

Coming Home

As I trek across the towering hills
I have only my own company in this vast country.
The journey home is far-reaching and tortoise-like,
My legs barely sustain me.
The sea of parched grass is around me,
Snaking between my bare toes.
My sore feet are swamped in blisters,
As though the plague has come again.

Finally the journey's over,
School's elapsed for one more day,
I've traipsed another mile,
But there's nobody here to say:
'Daniel, move yourself! We're ready to go out.'
My parents are blurred memories
Like worn photographs on the mantlepiece.
I stare at imprisoning walls
And prepare for another night
With the sleepless ghost of memory.

Daniel Compton (14)
Cecil Jones High School

England: London

London, the greatest city of them all,
Everything is there,
Even the Albert Hall.
With all the busy people running around,
In which disappears the traffic sound.
The old monuments that have been there for centuries,
Like the Tower of London.

I can't forget the old city of London,
Even when it was in ruins back in the war.
Even since then I have seen,
That this city is still strong,
It will keep the good and bad memories.
But who can forget Buckingham Palace,
Where in the heart of London lives
The Royal Family?

To finish off, last but not least,
The Thames river which flows through London,
Which has been there since London began.
New buildings have been built year by year,
But no one can forget the old city of London.

Hannah Axcell (15)
Cecil Jones High School

Home At Last

I am today, far away
Longing for my house, my home.
This feeling deep inside
Is like one I've never known.

But in my mind,
I'm home again,
Returned to Prittlewell
To this place I love,
Which means so much.

Graham Fuller (14)
Cecil Jones High School

THE FOOTBALL STADIUM

A football pitch full of thick, black mud,
Lots of smelly, sweaty socks,
Falling heavy,
The cats and dogs,
The rain doesn't stop.
Flooding the pitch one by one they sprint on.
Then it comes to the final breath,
The final kick,
The pitch is dim.
Scared and unnoticed the horror draws you in.
Free to breathe again, to the back of the net the ball shoots in.
The day is swallowed into the night,
The fans fall out of the stadium
And take over the tubes.
Pathways are swimming with smiling faces
And pubs are packed out with daring drunks.
But the stadium is left behind all deserted
With not a soul in sight.

Samantha Boxall (16)
Cecil Jones High School

About The Seasons . . .

In winter, the snowballs are darting,
Snowmen building and children laughing.
Fields cloaked in a thick frosted blanket;
No more playing in the frozen sandpit.

In autumn, Buckingham Palace is covered in leaves,
And past Big Ben, there is a gentle breeze,
Warm woollies, scarves and hats;
Diving into raked leaves perhaps.

In the spring, the pretty daisies are blooming,
Slugs eating flowers making gardeners fuming!
Days getting longer and beautiful sunsets;
Children fishing with little coloured nets.

In the summer the pier is full,
And the sheep get sheared for their fluffy wool,
Water fights and ice creams are all around,
In England a laugh is a wonderful sound.

Samantha Saunders (12)
Cecil Jones High School

England Ever Free

What is it about you that makes us feel so proud?
Crowds and crowds adore you,
Our anthem sung with pride.

The green fields and the forests protect us from harm,
This green and pleasant land
Has everlasting charm.

The men that gave their lives to keep this country free,
We remember them with pride -
The freedom gained for me.

The future of this country is up to you and me
So keep it just the way it is -
Our England . . . ever free.

Thomas Jarvis (12)
Cecil Jones High School

NUMBER 1 ENGLAND FAN

Come on England, we are in the World Cup!
Let's play the best football and never give up.
Come on England, and score loads of goals,
A free kick from Beckham, a volley from Scholes.

A tap in by Owen, a header from Sol,
We don't care who gets it in, just give us a goal.
Come on England, we've done it before;
You never know, one day Heskey might score!

Come on England, we know that you can,
So bring the World Cup home from Japan.
We know that we have the best football team,
So go out and play for country and Queen.

And if we should win it, I'm sure you will see
A much bigger party than for the Queen's Jubilee.
So 'Come on England!' we'll all shout out loud,
Go on and win it and make us all proud.

Terry Millington (13)
Cecil Jones High School

The England Witches' Spell

Three witches met upon a heath
To cast a spell to create a country
Full of happiness and love.

They were up all night finding the right ingredients;
Blue candles, red candles, crystals
And whatever else was in their book.

The first witch coughed into the cauldron,
And the second added too much water,
The third witch dipped her toe in,
And added too much mortar.

The country is now dirty and wet,
With uniforms and too many roads.
So the careless witches named it England;
And that's the way the story goes.

Krystine Gallagher (14)
Cecil Jones High School

England Is A Golden Ray

England is a golden ray
Glittering sand and the beauty of the bay
The sensational smell of freshly cut grass
Is a breath of fresh air on a warm summer's day.

England is a beautiful sunflower
Showing off its pride
Butterflies are stunning paintings
Floating around in the air.

English people are busy ants
With no time on their hands
They are a group of planets
Trying to orbit the sun.

The scent of fresh coffee beans
Fills the air in the morning's early hours
The tall architectural buildings
Stand with contempt and pride.

Jade Morris (14)
Cecil Jones High School

SOUTHEND-ON-SEA

From modern building to pretty park,
Amusement arcades, shops and sea.
Clubs that come alive at dark,
Surely this is the place to be.

From ancient church to fish and chips,
Pebbly shores to painted beach hut,
A walk on the pier to watch the ships,
Adventure playground pitch and putt.

Illuminations, Kursaal and carnival parade
Cinemas, theatres and the shops,
Watch seaside rock being made,
Break the law and meet the cops.

Open-topped buses and speedy trains,
Let people visit by the score.
May Bank Holiday, watch the planes,
To the town the crowds will pour.

Jessica Boxall (14)
Cecil Jones High School

Coming Home

Paralysed in a hurricane of choices and questions
Irritatingly trapped in a small cage
Time lingers as we ski along the monstrous oceans
Feeling every long-lasting minute, as I change age,
Puzzled by objects put on my lap -
Shall I eat it, or dissect it?
I just can't wait to get out of this abnormal snakepit.

Wide, wandering roads lead me to my humble home
Bitter scent of winter races with the howling wind
Bare, brown bark cheers me as I make my entrance
Unforgettable moonlight puts me in the spotlight
As the great show comes to a halt.

Hayley Watts (14)
Cecil Jones High School

England Is

Three lions on a shirt, with all the names gleaming
A diamond in a rock, will never stop me dreaming.

A star within a deep, dark sky,
A sky of one thousand smiles.
The queen within a continent,
Judges facing trials.

A needle in a haystack,
A love beyond life,
A husband without a wife.
St George's Cross waving in the breeze.

Leanne Hodgson (14)
Cecil Jones High School

SOUTHEND-ON-SEA

Southend-on-Sea, the place to be!
A garden show for the Royal Horticultural Society.
It was called Southend by Land, Air and Sea.

Southend has gardens and parks
And a sea that has no sharks.
A promenade on which to walk
And a beach where you can sit and talk.

Cycle paths, bowling and restaurants too,
A very long pier from which to view.
An air show that's second to none,
Where everyone can have some fun.

Don't take my word for it,
Come and see.
Southend-on-Sea -
The place to be!

Peter Martin (15)
Cecil Jones High School

THE QUEEN

Amidst her shining armour, among her jewels of time,
In a tower full of riches, she dreams of little crime.
With her three sons behind her and her daughter by her side,
She'll rule over land and country, with her utmost, deepest pride.
Her good friend, Jack, flies in the breeze, above her glamorous life,
With dukes and lords and countrymen, she's England's only wife.
And with her fans behind her, 'God Save The Queen' is sung,
And she knows deep within her heart, that soon her job is done.

Jenny Metcalfe (15)
Cecil Jones High School

Southend Sorrow

Southend is full of sorrow,
As the crows and birds of fear
Prey upon this lonely town
Like a lion upon a zebra.

A grim face hangs upon Southend
Like the Grim Reaper
Hangs upon his duty.

People all around look for hope,
But all hope fails
As it swirls into an abyss,
Like a whirlpool devouring a ship.

Adam Thorogood (15)
Cecil Jones High School

My Best Friend

My best friend
is just like me
she likes jelly
and strawberry ice cream.

My best friend
has ginger hair
but I don't care.

My best friend
will stay with me
especially when I'm sad.

My best friend
will stick up for me
when people bully me bad.

Holly Fordham (11)
Chafford Hundred Campus

The Seat

There is a cab
that is blue
and is haunted
by a boy.

In the silence
of the day.

The driver looks
in the mirror
and sees a body
lying there, still.

In the silence
of the day.

He looks back,
there's no one
there, but a
puddle of blood.

Then it goes
with a gunshot
heard.

In the silence
of the day.

But there
is no blood,
no cab, no driver
and no life,
until the day
is silent.

Matthew Tansley (12)
Chafford Hundred Campus

I Am

I am friend.
I am very loving to a fish.

I am fish.
I am very loving to a friend.

I am a friend to fish
I am very loving.

A loving friend to 'I am, I am'
Very fish.

Loving to 'Am I fish?
Am I?' - a very friend.

Fish to a friend!
Am I loving? Am I very?

Friend fish! I am
I am loving to a 'very'.

I am to very loving fish
Am I a friend.

Natasha Lane (11)
Chafford Hundred Campus

Hands Of A Baby

Babies' hands
The size of a raindrop
Delicate like glass
Smooth as a ray's belly.

Babies' hands
Soft as sponge
Clenched like a boxer's fist
Always being sucked.

Charles Dack (11)
Chafford Hundred Campus

I Am A Sportsman

I am a sportsman.
I am very good at rugby.

I am rugby.
I am very good at a sportsman.

I am a sportsman at rugby.
I am very good.

A good sportsman at 'I am, I am.'
Very good.

Good at 'Am I rugby?
Am I?' - A very sportsman.

Rugby at a sportsman.
Am I good? Am I very?

Sportsman rugby! I am.
I am good at a 'very'.

I am at very good rugby!
Am I a sportsman?

James Johnson (11)
Chafford Hundred Campus

I Am A Writer

I am a writer.
I am very good at writing.

I am writing.
I am very good at a writer.

I am a writer at a writing.
I am very good.

A good writer at 'I am, I am,'
Very writing.

Good at 'Am I writing?
Am I?' A very writer.

Writing at a writer
Am I good? Am I very?

Writer, writing I am.
I am good at a very.

I am at very good writing.
Am I a writer?

Connor Grover (11)
Chafford Hundred Campus

My Hamster

My hamster
Is totally, utterly gross,
His spinner is a winner
But full of droppings.

On to my dressing table, they fall
And I really do not like it at all,
He wees in the corner,
That is so out of order.

His droppings look like chocolate peanuts,
His wheel sounds like a mouse in distress,
I really wish he would give it a rest,
His noise is like a classroom of screaming children.

His gnawing is not applauding,
He gnaws on his cage in utter rage,
He is white and may give you a fright,
His little hands are like baby shells in the sands.

Riya Bernard (11)
Chafford Hundred Campus

The Dog And The Potatoes

I am a dog.
I am extra kind to potatoes.

I am potatoes.
I am extra kind to a dog.

I am a dog to potatoes.
I am extra kind.

A dog to 'I am, I am'
Extra potatoes!

Kind of 'I am a dog
Am I?' - Extra potatoes.

Potatoes of a dog!
Am I extra! Am I kind?

Dog potatoes! I am.
I am extra to a 'kind'.

I am of extra kind potatoes!
Am I a dog?

Andrew Woollard (12)
Chafford Hundred Campus

My Rabbit

He sits in his hutch,
Waiting,
Looks out and watches,
Waiting,
A door swings open,
Waiting,
They've got a bowl,
Waiting,
He starts hopping about,
Waiting,
His hutch door opens,
Waiting,
He tucks in and then
Relief!

Another day goes,
Waiting,
The door swings open,
Waiting,
There's a box,
Waiting,
The hutch door opens,
Waiting,
And then, oh no!
He sits there staring,
Waiting,
He thinks,
Waiting,
And they start playing,
Waiting no more!

Claire Dale (12)
Chafford Hundred Campus

Do Not Forget Your Bicycle Hat

I left for school,
My mum wagged her finger,
She warned, 'Do not linger
And do not forget your bicycle hat!'

I grabbed my bikc
And I got on my way,
'I'll wear my bike helmet another day.'
And that was that.

'No bike helmet for me,
It's not trendy or cool,
I'm no idiot or fool.'
And that was that.

It started to shower,
My foot became wet and unsteady,
About to fall I was not ready
And that was that.

Out of control,
I crashed onto the pavement,
My head got a painful dent
And that was that.

I picked myself up,
With my wounds in pain,
Then I walked my bike home in the rain
And that was that.

Feeling sorry for myself,
Clothes covered in mud,
My face smeared with blood,
I wish I wore my bicycle hat!

Aaron Smith (12)
Chafford Hundred Campus

THE MONKEY

I am a monkey
I am really interested in a monkey

I am ants
I am really interested in a monkey

I am a monkey in ants
I am really interested

An interested monkey 'I am, I am'
Really ants

Interested in 'Am I ants
Am I?' - A really monkey

Ants in a monkey
Am I interested? Am I really?

Monkey ants! I am
I am interested in a really!

I am really interested in ants!
Am I a monkey.

Scott Hyland (11)
Chafford Hundred Campus

BUILDER'S HAND

Builder's hands.
Rough as splintered wood.
Broad as a metal pole.
Dirty like wet soil.

Builder's hands.
Red raw like burnt skin.
Hard like dry cement.
Hands grip like a hard metal vice.

Andrew Dark (11)
Chafford Hundred Campus

I Am

I am a chef,
I am extremely caring to cars.

I am cars,
I am extremely caring to a chef.

I am chef to cars,
I am extremely caring.

A caring chef 'I am, I am,'
Extremely cars.

Cars to a chef!
Am I caring, am I extremely?

Caring to 'Am I cars,
Am I?' - extremely chef.

Chef cars! I am
I am caring, 'extremely'.

I am to extremely caring cars,
Am I a chef.

Brogan Connolly (11)
Chafford Hundred Campus

My Best Friend

My best friend
She has brown hair
She has brown eyes
She has a brother just like I.

My best friend
She likes strawberry milkshake
She likes ice cream
She likes Twixs just like I.

My best friend
She is kind
She is nice
She likes chocolate
She likes spice
My best friend she is.

My best friend
She is mad
But she makes me happy
When I'm sad.

Amy Blundell (11)
Chafford Hundred Campus

The Eagle

The dark-faced weapon with his fierce temper
Darts down like a thunderbolt to the ground,
He swoops down using his claws and bludgeoning beak as hands,
He grabs and catches, he acts like a bloodthirsty cannibal.

Charlie Court (12)
Chafford Hundred Campus

THE GORILLA

I am a gorilla
I am absolutely nuts about bananas.

I am a banana
I am absolutely nuts about gorillas.

I am bananas to a gorilla
I am absolutely nuts.

I am absolutely nuts I am, I am
Very bananas.

Bananas of a gorilla
I am absolutely, I am nuts.

Gorilla bananas I am, I am
Absolutely nuts of very.

I am a gorilla of bananas
Absolutely nuts am I.

Joseph Leonardi (11)
Chafford Hundred Campus

UNDER THE SEA

Mermaids swimming under the sea
where all the shells will be,
shells laying in the palm of the hand
as I see rocks among the sand.

The odd pebbles under the sea
the fishes swimming underneath me.

Hollie Willmot (11)
Chafford Hundred Campus

My Poem

I am a model
I am really interested in boys.

I am boys
I am really interested in a model.

I am a model of boys
I am interested really.

I am interested in a model
'Really, really' interested.

Really 'Am I a boy?'
Am I? - an interested model!

Boys of a model.
'Am I interested? Am I really?'

Model boys I am!
'I am interested in a really?'

I am a boy
Am I a really interested model?

Abbi Reid (11)
Chafford Hundred Campus

Friends

Friends are special people
They always stay with you

In joy and in sadness
They share those times with you

If you give them something
Then they will repay

If they go knock for you and you say no,
They'll go away but come again another day.

Colin Moy (11)
Chafford Hundred Campus

I Am A Boy

I am a boy.
I am extremely desperate for sleep.

I am sleep.
I am extremely desperate for a boy.

I am a boy for sleep.
Extremely desperate, I am.

An extremely desperate boy for sleep
I am . . . I am.

Desperate for sleep, extremely I am,
I am a boy.

Boy for sleep
I am, I am extremely desperate!

I am for sleep
I am an extremely desperate boy.

I am extremely desperate for sleep.
Am I a boy?

Shaan Patel (12)
Chafford Hundred Campus

My Family

My mum is quicker than a twister,
She never gets a blister,
She likes to cook
But she doesn't like the Harry Potter book.

My dad is a computer freak,
But he loves to eat,
He makes me laugh
When he's daft.

My sister is a show-off,
Hopefully it will wear off,
She's already eight
And she's never late.

My brother likes to fight,
'Cause he's training to be a knight,
He likes to play his secret game,
But he doesn't like his name.

My family is normal,
They're always formal,
They don't like tea,
But they do love me.

Celen Hurbas (13)
Chafford Hundred Campus

Someone, Somewhere

Someone, Somewhere
Dreams of your smile
While thinking of you
Has made my living worthwhile

Some when you're alone
Remember it's true
Somewhere I'll always
Be thinking of you!

Kymberley Jamieson (12)
Chafford Hundred Campus

Baby's Face

Baby's face
Like a prawn
All crinkled and wrinkled
All red and peachy.

Baby's face
Her eyes are the blue sea
Shining up at me
With a slight gleam.

Baby's face
Her nose is as small as a 5p
A button; it is all red and shiny
It's very round
But yet it must grow to a £1.

Baby's face
Her mouth is so small
But when she opens it
It is as loud as a trumpet.

Baby's face
Like a prawn
All crinkled and wrinkled
All red and peachy.

Abigail Hawkins (11)
Chafford Hundred Campus

My Poem

I am a twirler,
Am I a very good twirler?

A twirler am I,
A very good twirler I am.

A very good twirler
'I am, I am' a twirler.

I am a good twirler,
I am a very twirler.

A very twirler I am,
Am I a good twirler?

A very good twirler am I,
I am a twirler.

A very good twirler am I,
Am I a twirler?

Charlotte Cullen (11)
Chafford Hundred Campus

Autumn Time

The golden trees are starting to turn,
with the moist dew settling in the morning sun.
Crispy leaves on the road,
dark in the morning when no one's about.
Out in the chilly morning you can see your breath
hanging there like little crystals,
enjoy it while you can!

Aaron Merrigan (12)
Chafford Hundred Campus

Autumn Leaves

Who's that buzzing among the leaves?
I said a bee.

Who's that singing among the leaves?
I said a bird.

Who's that looking for nuts among the leaves?
I said a squirrel.

Who's that making a bed among the leaves?
I said a hedgehog.

Who's that playing among the leaves?
I said a child.

Frankie Howe (11)
Chafford Hundred Campus

Autumn

Crisp brown leaves gently float to the ground as they fall
Tall trees stand proud as they tower over the dew-covered grass.
The birds chirp their soothing lullaby
As the soft buds of flowers dangle in the cool breeze.

The warming sun spreads an even glow over the golden forest
And the light twinkles through the trees.
Burrowing squirrels gather nuts ready for winter.
Climbing trees.

Flowers blooming, birds chirping, leaves falling, squirrels hiding,
These are all the signs of autumn.

Ashley Watson (12)
Chafford Hundred Campus

SCHOOL

School, school is cool,
When it's like a swimming pool,
Speeding past maths,
Splashing through art,
You're gonna whizz through it
Like a fast gone go-kart.

The teachers are mean,
Like an old wicked queen,
The teachers that are kind,
Are the ones you should find.

When it's half term,
Say hip hip hooray!
But just remember
You had a great day!

Jeffrey Huynh (11)
Chafford Hundred Campus

MY DOG

My dog's called Sandy
And she loves chasing cats.
Next door's got a cat
That's her fave.

She runs around the hay field,
Running all about,
Jumping, leaping, barking along,
Chasing this little cat.

She stays there for hours,
But comes back when she's hungry,
Which is a real pain
Because I have to brush the hay
Out of her soft fur.

My dog loves chasing cats
And I love her!

Robyn Freeman (12)
Chafford Hundred Campus

I'M A FOOTBALLER

I am a footballer,
I am good at shooting balls.

I am good at shooting balls,
I am a footballer.

I am a footballer,
Am I good at shooting balls?

I am balls shooting,
A footballer at am I good.

At balls shooting I am good,
I am a footballer.

I'm good at balls at shooting,
I am a footballer.

Am I good at shooting balls?
Am I a footballer?

Jamie Hanks (11)
Chafford Hundred Campus

A Dream Goal

On Saturday I played football,
It was even better than being at school.
I scored a goal, fell down a hole
And everyone jumped on top of me.

When I sat up and looked around,
People were cheering around the ground.
My mates were shouting, 'Get up, get up!
Cos now we've won the big gold cup!'

I looked towards the stand and saw
A shiny cup with ribbons galore,
To lift that cup has been my dream
And now I'm lifting it for my team.

They lifted me up into the air,
They sat the cup upon my hair.
We ran to the other end of the ground,
Our mums and dads were jumping around.

All of a sudden I heard a shout,
My mum was calling, 'Get out, get out!'
I turned around and bumped my head,
On the bedpost of my bed.

It was only a dream after all,
So I got straight up and took my ball.
After breakfast, to the park I ran,
To train for the match where we'll win again.

Steven Blake (12)
Chafford Hundred Campus

Christmas Day

On Christmas Day,
I came down to see
Lots of presents
Waiting for me.

I unwrapped the paper
And then I saw
Lots of new clothes
To put in my drawer.

Some new underwear,
I had to laugh,
Then my mum called me up
For a morning bath.

Christmas pudding,
I couldn't wait,
I hurried to get dressed
I couldn't be late.

The Christmas tree
Seemed so tall,
If I knocked it
It would fall.

Next Christmas Day
Another beer,
I can't wait
'Til next year.

Emily Higgs (11)
Chafford Hundred Campus

DOLPHINS

As shiny as stars
As fast as cars
As clever as scientists
As smooth as silk.

As blue as the sky
As round as a pie
Their speak is like a cry
They don't want to die.

Will I see one
Having fun?
I hope I will,
I wish I will.

Roseanne Howard (11)
Chafford Hundred Campus

BABY'S HANDS

Baby hands
Small like a butterfly
Soft and silky like a feather
Wrinkly like Chinese sharps

Baby's hands
All screwed up like a ball
As tiny as a small snowball
Like puppy's paws, all smooth and velvety

Always sucking their thumbs
With little fingernails as inched as can be.
Faint lifelines that you can hardly see.

Jasmin Skeet (11)
Chafford Hundred Campus

SCHOOL

School, the place where everybody hates to go,
The place where all the children dread,
The place where all the teachers shout,
It's the place where everybody hates to go.

Before school starts there is already a fight,
Between years 9 and 10!
One of them is tempted to bite.
Punches and kicks being thrown around
And then one of the little 'uns!
But is soon stopped by the big year 11's
And the playground is so silent without them.
All of the two classes are in for detention,
For the next two terms!

Ranvir Singh Bhogal (13)
Cranbrook College

CHRISTMAS

Christmas is a celebration.
It is fun putting up lights and a tree,
Children often wait for Santa
And put out cookies and milk.

There is some snow
And we throw snowballs and slush,
We get wet and filthy you can bet.

In Christmas we get into a bunch
And eat Christmas lunch.
There is turkey and roast,
That is what I like most.

Marcus Dyal (12)
Cranbrook College

THE LAST BREATH

With all this extra pressure, the question I wonder is
After death, after my last breath, will I ever get to rest from my obsessions.
They punish the people asking questions;
And those who possess, steal from those without possessions.
Make sure you always study all your lessons,
Even the genius asks his questions,
Be grateful for blessings, the power is in the people we address,
Always do your best and don't ever settle for less.
Never let the pressure make you panic
And when you get stranded,
And things don't ever go the way you planned it.
I can't stop dreaming of riches
And I'm never in the position to make a difference,
And if I go insane, it's simply the lack of fame,
I'm never going to change;
Life's nothing but a game.

After I die, after the final blink of my eye,
I won't ever have to ride this world anymore,
The only thing I have to achieve
Is to make sure my family never become poor.
And keep all the little kids way clear of all the mischief.
The message I strive to make -
Keep all of your loved ones near to you,
And all your hated clear of you,
Never con anyone with something fake,
By doing this you're just declaring your desired fate.
If you decide not to listen,
You'll just be cursing yourself when in prison.
I hope you take the right turning
Because if you don't you will be sent down to Hell the burning.

Alex Deakin (14)
Cranbrook College

The Ways Of The World

Money is mandatory, my ways are self-explanatory,
I try hard and proceed to tell my horrid stories,
I'm in too deep, all my friends, bring them shovel stories,
Some people strapped with their guns, trying to kill my family,
Ways of the world, how will I last when the economy crashes,
I'm going all out getting my cash,
While spend mine open, with my eyes on the world,
People in jail cells gave me stories to tell,
My body swells from the evil smells that I inhale,
Evil sets me up to fail, make my life so real.

They say I look just like my father, without the beard,
They should have named him, magic he disappears,
A couple of months out of the year, he reappears,
It's all the same, ain't nothing changed, you're still my father,
Don't hold a grudge, just show me love,
I'm on my own, I'm kind of sober from a broken home,
Wondering what's going on, did I deserve this,
Living in these hard times got me really scared and nervous,
My mother tried to feed us all, until she got laid off,
Now we're all laid off.

Even though it hurts my chest I'm going to try till I lose my breath,
Looking to sin since life began,
Coming all the way out the water to get oxygen,
Please Father help me breathe again, at ease again,
When you close your eyes, can you state the pain, the misery,
Hoping that you will rescue me,
These are the ways of the world,
Now I have to choose between life or losing my sanity,
Stay away from the streets,
Keep calling me,
These are the ways of the world.

Sagar Desai (14)
Cranbrook College

RATS

I hate rats,
Nasty little pests,
They are even worse than bats,
During the night they never take any rests.

They are big
And very ugly,
They eat like pigs
And they are very fat for their size.

Every night they look in your garbage,
I think they are scavengers,
They search for the leftovers of your past meals
And their waste falls onto your bins!

Rats come in different colours and sizes,
Some are brown and some are grey,
The small ones are thin and fast,
But I hate the one which is black and fat.

To get rid of a rat,
Get a cat,
Put the cat next to the rats' homes
And watch them being slaughtered.

Benoy Soman (11)
Cranbrook College

MY DREAM

In my dream I like to not be seen for purposes as fights.
In my dream there is no cause of any hectic war
In my dream it's safe and sound where peace is upon us all.
I always dream that I speak in front of a huge and giant crowd,
A speech of thanks, forgiveness, peace and where war is not found.

In my dream there is no room for bloodthirsty little gangs
In my dream there are people who are normal and are not killing fans.
They come from places near and far,
Counties, countries and even stars, which really is quite far.

Timothy Lee (11)
Cranbrook College

LEARNING FROM HIP-HOP MUSIC

The music is different,
When you hear it you shrink,
As the singers that rap it,
Doesn't matter what they say,
Doesn't matter how they look,
Ironically though,
Most actually look good.

Hip-hop has definitely
Made people rise,
But sadly however,
It's made some die.
An example of this
And he always uses boast
Is Tupac Shakur,
Who ruled the west coast.

The most important thing however,
Is simply what you think,
You might not like hip-hop,
You might think it stinks.
But in life you should always do.
This is advise and a fact,
Is to first see and think,
And then commit your act.

Michael Khoshdel (14)
Cranbrook College

Heroes

This world holds tonnes of heroes
Fictional, non-fictional, sci-fi, who cares?
But has anyone ever cared
Who they really are?
It's an easy question - isn't it?

You have Batman, Superman and Spidey
Lazy twerps swinging around alleys
Trying to catch villains single-handed
What good is that
When you have tonnes of 'em?

Then you have groups like the X-Men
They're not so bad,
Until one of them has a real bust-up
You start seeing huge cracks in 'em.

Next up you have Odysseus and Hercules
But they all have an Achilles heel
- A real waste of time and space.

Sci-fi heroes are totally rubbish
The thought of it is grubbish
As there are no alien 'heroes'.

The real heroes are always alive
They live in this big beehive
The thing we call Earth.

Doctors, policemen, soldiers,
Yes, you know whom
But do you make them heroic enough?

So there you have it, the true tale
Even everyone can now agree
Even Eminem's better than Superman etc,
Which leads me to - villains!

Naseer Hayath (12)
Cranbrook College

THE WRITER OF THIS GENIUS POEM

(Based on 'The Writer Of This Poem' by Roger McGough)

The writer of this poem,
Is taller than a pine tree,
As keen as the south wind,
As handsome as can be.

As bold as a boxing glove,
As sharp as a knife blade,
As strong as scaffolding
And doesn't like marmalade.

As smooth as a cherry,
As quick as a lick,
As clean as a chemist shop,
As clever as a . . .

The writer of this poem
Never ceases to amaze,
He's one in a million billion, trillion
(Or so the poem says!)

P.S. To finish off
The writer of this poem
Is Albert Einstein!

Zubair Altaf (11)
Cranbrook College

Oh, To Be Warm

As I stand at the bus stop,
Waiting for what seems like hours,
I dream of summer and flowers
Where it is warm and children play.

Still, I wait for the bus,
Oh how I hope
As I watch the paper boy mope,
How does he cope?

Finally the bus comes,
My heart's beating like a drum
Because it is so cold,
I wish I were more bold.

I get on the bus
And the warmth hits me
While I pay my fee,
I am full of glee!

As I welcome the heat
I notice, there are no seats!
As the bus pulls away,
I begin my day.

Ian Gregory (15)
Cranbrook College

The Wheel

Through wintertime we call on spring
And through the spring on summer call
And when complete hedges ring
Declare that winter's best of all;

And after that there's nothing good
Because the springtime has not come -
Nor know that what bothers our blood
Is but its longing for the tomb.

Nilesh Bodalia (14)
Cranbrook College

POEM

I woke up in the morning, hey man!
Not looking forward to school, cos borin'.
Still tired and began to yawn
My dad's in the car beepin' the horn. *Beep! Beep!*

We go in and do some writing
Something wrong with the room, it's the lighting.
We get it wrong we hear a yell
What out it's Mr Buck.

We get our dinner and huddle in a bunch
Sandwiches, bananas and chips for lunch
Mr Buck with his lunch too,
Sneak to his yoghurt and add some shampoo.

The bell goes and we make a run
We go to the park and have some fun
It's then time for a sleep, yeh fatsoes.
I woke up in the mornin' to a *beep, beep, beep.*
Oh! Get away I'm still sleeping.

Adding shampoo
Beepin' the horn
Hey Mr Buck, this poem's for you.

Farhaan Akoo (12)
Cranbrook College

The Creature

It lurks behind the tall grass and trees!
Hungry for blood it'll eat anything it sees!
It waits for something to come in its path!
It'll pounce on it and give it a blood bath!

It rips and tears all the pieces!
Still hungry so looks for the deer's nieces!
He didn't know it would give him grief!
Saw the hunter take the sword out of the sheath!

It roared and it whimpered, ran as fast as he could!
It was startled and terrified as it stood!
It pounced at the hunter with everything he had
Shot it in the stomach with a super deadly dart!

But who knows when the creature
Will strike again!

Ashfaaq Patel (13)
Cranbrook College

Magical Water

Magical water so deep and blue,
Magical ocean so clean and blue;
Sharks and whales gather together,
When they're tired they sleep in a feather.

Singing water so beautiful,
Horrible water so miserable;
Gifts of rain
Holly drifting from the river.

Stars drawn on the sky,
Waves drawn in ocean and sea;
Beautiful waves so nice and gentle,
Pavements made of mud.

Gurnam Chagar (11)
Cranbrook College

My Mind

Delve deep into my mind
And make amazing finds.
Don't mind the mess
It's Carl Anka brand, the best.

Here it is in its entire splendour
I try to fight it but normally surrender.
It's the department for computer games
My parents don't know it exists so don't mention any names.

This part is so wonderful I even enjoy describing it
It's the number one smash hit.
It's the fun section, full of jokes and laughs
Laugh so badly you'll fall in half.

But now alas the laugh has gone
Because it's the hate department we are now upon.
Unsavoury characters, school and homework
And a woman with a big fat, evil smirk.

These are the most notable things in my mind
But there are many secrets left for you to find.
Dare you delve deeper and take a look?
No, you mustn't and I must close this book.

Carl Anka (11)
Cranbrook College

FOOTBALL

The score is 1-0
Blues are in front, reds are behind.
Come on boys, come on boys!
Show them what you're made of, made of,
Made of, show them what you're made of.

Beckham's in front, Owen's behind,
Beckham kicks the ball, it's an Owen goal.
The equaliser, the equaliser!

It's the beginning of the second half,
The second half has started, good for the reds,
Come on boys, come on boys!

The blues are attacking, attacking, attacking,
As the board comes up our substitute Fowler comes on
Everybody applauds, Fowler, Fowler!

Ah! It's Fowler, he passes to Owen
And he scores! Owen scored! Owen scored!

The final whistle blows, whistle blows
And England have done it again!

Mohammed Kothia (12)
Cranbrook College

HALLOWE'EN

See the pumpkin fat and round
Lying on the cold, wet ground.
Now look up in the moonlit sky
And you will see the bats that fly.
Look oh so cheerful - ghosts can be seen
Because this night is Hallowe'en.

Amarjeet Singh Sohal (14)
Cranbrook College

THAT LOVE

I'm that light when you can't see
I'm that air when you can't breathe
I'm that feeling when you can't leave
Some doubt, some lie, some cheat.

When you're weak I make you strong,
Here's where you belong,
I ain't perfect but I promise I will never do you wrong,
Keep you away from harm,
My love is protected, I'll wrap you in my arms
So you never feel neglected.

I want to make you aware,
What we had was rare,
At the moment of despair,
I'm that courage when you scare,
Loyal,
Down for you,
Soon as I saw you,
Wanted to be there 'cause I couldn't hold it down for you,
Be around for you,
Plant seeds in the soil,
Make love all night, bend them bed coils,
You're a queen, therefore I treat you royal,
This is all for you,
'cause I simply adore you.

Saliya Jayaweera (14)
Cranbrook College

PLEASE SON, DON'T BUY NO GUN

When I was young
Mama told me, 'Please Son, don't buy no gun.'
I didn't realise life's about having fun.
Until I saw my boy get done.
A twelve-year-old getting hit by shells from a gun.
I should've listened to Ma and not act like a clown,
I'm sure the way I acted made the all-knowing frown.
But now I say, 'No more!' because I've unshut my eyes
And the difference between God's word and man's wills was realised.
Seeing opposing parallel lives some liquid, others frozen.
Let me never seek from man what God has chosen
Now across my face is a brand new smile.
With a newly revealed meaning of a fortunate child
Why am I a fortunate child?
Because I made off the streets
I just hope that my unborn child
Will take this to heart more than I did
'Please Son, don't buy no gun.'

To all my fallen soldiers.

Matthew Patterson-Muir (14)
Cranbrook College

FANTASY LAND

The fantasy land has just arrived,
A land with everything you can imagine.
Chocolate trees and liquorice chairs
And even marshmallow marshes.

Minty rulers and sugary houses,
Creamy tissues and chocolately scissors.
But even better then everything here,
A skyscraper filled with toys and games.

Card games and board games,
But best of all, the video games of course!
All the video games you could think of were there
PlayStation, Gamecube and XBox.

But of course all this must end
When I heard a familiar ringing.
I opened my eyes and sat up in bed
Before I switched my alarm off.

Rahul Ravalia (11)
Cranbrook College

SEASONS

Fireworks go *boom,*
Little children run to their room.
The leaves fall,
The trees look tall.

Cold as ice,
Nobody nice.
Christmas is here,
Santa and reindeer.

Spring,
Phones ring,
Summer's on the way,
Hooray, hooray, hooray.

It is very hot,
People go out a lot.
The sun shines so bright,
There is more daylight.

The holidays are here,
Children cheer.

Sukhdeep Sangha (11)
Cranbrook College

The Game

Chess, chess, the game is constructive,
In this game nobody is disruptive.
This board has squares of sixty-four,
Within this there is a war.

Thirty-two black squares, thirty-two white,
Bishops, rooks, queens and knights.
Then the war starts, there is a fight,
The opponents rage, with all their might.

The object of the game, to keep your king,
How good are you? That's the thing!
Most of these pieces will be killed,
In this brilliant game, you should be thrilled.

The powerful queen, she is the terminator,
Soon the other pieces will learn to love or hate her.
Black or white, saint or sinner,
In the game there is only one winner.

In the game you can dominate,
Or just lose pitifully, *checkmate!*

Arvind Nair (13)
Cranbrook College

The Tramp

He is the tramp, ruthlessly ignored,
He is the tramp, lying in the cold,
Scrounging change for his food,
Nothing will change his lonely mood.
He tries and tries, but can never succeed
To provide for his necessary needs.

What he wants, he will not get
Neither will his needs ever set.
Yet still, do they toil and toil
But never get, what they deserve from the soil.
Needs are satisfied not
They are and always will be forgot.

Rizwan Syed (13)
Cranbrook College

A Mysterious Shark

A mysterious shark waiting to be fed,
With deep blue eyes,
Lying under the sea bed.

A mysterious shark has no fear,
With deep blue eyes,
Waiting to appear.

A mysterious shark
With deep blue eyes,
Leaving his bloody mark.

A mysterious shark sees his prey,
With deep blue eyes,
This will make his day.

Finally the shark gets his prey,
This would certainly make his day,
The vicious beast is mysterious
To the seas he is a curse.

Piyush Patel (13)
Cranbrook College

THE SUPERCAR

A huge roar emits from four giant exhaust pipes,
Creating a haze of dense and choking smoke.
The tyres let out a shriek as the machine begins its journey.
My jaw drops as the car races up the road,
Seeming to be attempting to reach the horizon.
For this is no ordinary car,
Its sleek lines ooze intent and speed,
This is a Lamborghini.
At top speed, the roar is deafening
And shudders run through you,
But I know it's worth it,
For sheer brute speed and excitement,
For adrenaline and pure joy,
Nothing can match it.
This is a Lamborghini.

Sunjay Bhudia (14)
Cranbrook College

DUCKS

There are a lot of ducks, that do not cluck
Because a cluck it lacks,
Instead it quacks,
It is very fond
Of a puddle and pond
And when it dines
It turns upside down.
It likes bread,
Has a small head
And makes its bed on shore.

Nikesh Patel (12)
Cranbrook College

In School

It was my first day,
I walked through the gates,
I was scared and nervous,
I saw one of my mates.

I walked to him, I said, How are you doing?'
He said, 'Today is my last day and I am going.'
He showed me round the school
And also he showed me the school pool.

The school was enormous
The lessons passed,
The end of the day bell rang
And the kids all sang.

I went on the 147 home to East Ham,
I saw my mum and told her what a day it was
Then I had dinner,
That was the end of my day.

Kishen Nakum (12)
Cranbrook College

Stars

Stars. They're our bright light.
Our personal small suns in the sky.
We see them come day or night,
They guide us when we are lost,
Shining their bright light upon our path,
They make us wish for glorious things in dark places,
Stars, they're our bright light.

Quikobad Hussain (14)
Cranbrook College

Three Little Wolves And The Big Bad Pig

It wasn't my fault the pig was cooked
The last time I looked,
He was above the chimney wall
You see this all,
Started when he came after us to eat us
We were all building houses
One of straw, one of sticks
And my own little house made out of bricks
Then the pig came walking by
And thought, that he would try
To munch us, for his supper
But we had other
Plans opposite from the pig
We decided that we needed to get rid
Of this thorn in our sides.
So we went inside, to devise a plan,
The pig came and said, 'Hey little wolf let me in.'
We said, 'Not by the hair of our chilli chin chin.'
So he huffed and puffed
But that was not enough
To blow the house down
He climbed up the chimney, just as we thought
And directly under the chimney, we put a boiling pot
And as he fell from the chimney, into it he got
So that was the end of our lovely friend
But as people stood by and dawdled,
They said, 'Fools!' for they saw a sign saying,
Beware of the big bad wolves.

Debo Adebayo (12)
Cranbrook College

Sometimes

Sometimes when I'm alone I cry,
I cry because I feel I am on my own.

The tears fall from my eyes, down my cheek,
The pains keep growing and still here to keep.
It's also hard to get to sleep,
When you know nightmares are all you seek.

The growing pains of waking up every day
I try not to remind myself that they are here to stay.
The thoughts of it all puts me in dismay.

People ask am I all right?
I smile, and hold it all in tight
And to their delight, let them hear what's right.

Will I die my life all alone?
Will my family and my friends all be gone?
I cry because my heart is torn.

But tell me who will stay and listen,
By the time I finish telling my story all of our souls would have risen.

Living life on this so called Earth,
Why couldn't I just have died before my birth?
Why must we all live a life of curse?

I need to come out of the pool of death,
I'll try my best,
To hold on and contest.

Now I have to choose between life or lose my sanity,
But it's hard when the streets keep calling me,
What will my future be?

Asfan Sheikh (14)
Cranbrook College

THE PANTHER

He glides through the forest
Making dents in the leaves,
He searches for his victim
Licking his lips
He is the panther in the night
The demon from Hell.

His yellow eyes flash,
Sending a chill through the trees,
Animals shiver
As they sense his unwanted presence,
He is the panther in the night
The demon from Hell.

I watch him through the bushes,
His movement,
His stare,
He gives a cry and sends out his message,
He has achieved his goal,
He is the panther in the night,
The demon from Hell.

Rinu Senan (12)
Cranbrook College

THE DRAGONFLY

I had a friend that is a dragonfly,
That flew all day in the sky,
He breathed fire
And loved the choir.

Every month, every day
He grew bigger and never thought that he'd pass away,
Every day was like a new day for him,
Until he crashed and lost his wing.

He dived down and hit his head,
Then suddenly he was dead,
Now he's gone I miss him so,
I wished his life wouldn't end in a blow.

Absher Mansoor (12)
Cranbrook College

Reaching

I was born in this world with no money,
I went hot summers and cold winters,
With no dinner and a freezer full of ice
Was nothing nice.
At first, to me, it really seemed funny,
But now I can see that I was really wrong,
So I got down to it,
I put my mind to it
And from then I knew that I couldn't quit,
Or I would just drop, straight into a bottomless pit.
I can't be stopped, I'm near the top,
I will never drop,
Because I'm still reaching high,
But on the way I made some people cry,
I had to lie.
I'll make it up to them,
To my family and closest friends,
I hope they forgive me and I can depend on them.
But till then I will still and always look over them,
As they set me free,
Lead me on the right path
And now I'm part of the right path.

Indveer Kataria (14)
Cranbrook College

The Tears Of Omaha

Boats flying into Omaha,
Iron-armed to the teeth,
Controlled by the rough sea,
Boats tilting, turning, sinking,
The beach drawing nearer.

The snipers at the mountain tops,
Showing no remorse as they shoot us, the green dots,
Breaking down the damaged forces,
Easy prey for the Nazis below.

The machine guns thundering through the mists of war,
The screams of hundreds falling to their deaths, vomiting blood,
The man in white with the red cross on his back
Trying his best to offer the dying soldiers the last rites.

The blasts of the grenades burning many nearby
As the few brave soldiers make it to the mountain screaming victory,
Lighting the flares,
The magnificent explosions go by.

Zeppelins slowly moving across the skies,
A gift from the heavens,
Destroying many friend and foe and only way to end the war.
I look up at the sky,
Only to see the massacre, the last bombs dropping by,
Dropping like the last tear from my eye.

Isuru Perera (13)
Cranbrook College

The War

Over the top I go, but stop my run
Only to see you still clutching your gun.
As I look at you with dismay
You are not the only one who lay.

As I stand here staring with my eyes
And yet still I hear more cries,
What is the point of this war?
Don't ask me, I'm not sure.

Davender Shergill (15)
Cranbrook College

THE ORPHAN

The poor old boy,
Discarded like a toy,
His parents away
And his cruel sister at bay.

His life is a struggle each and every day,
He met a thief all alone one day,
He had fear in his heart
And with the harsh world he didn't want to part.

He did as he was told,
When the day had grown old,
But he found his lover, a beautiful girl,
With whom he danced with, with a twirl and a whirl.

But she did not love him back,
For she was a widow and that was a fact,
His heart was shattered
And to him nothing really mattered.

His cruel sister had died
And his love was denied
And all that was left,
Was the cold hand of death.

Rajen Raniga (13)
Cranbrook College

The Quran

A book that is full of answers,
A book that makes you cry,
A book that makes you notice,
How much harder you can try.

A book that makes you realise,
What true love really is . . .
A book that gives you direction,
For all of life's tough biz.

A book that gives you hope,
That someone, somewhere's watching over you,
A book that helps you out,
Through all the times you're blue.

A book that was revealed to our beloved prophet (peace be upon Him),
Over a period of 23 years.
Once you put faith in this book,
You can handle worldly fears.

A gift sent out of Heaven,
A treasure from above,
Written proof that shows us
How blessed we are with the Lord Almighty's love.

Irfaan Karim (14)
Cranbrook College

Arrested

The police, they arrested me for speeding,
I would have been better off doing the gardening.
I pleaded with the officer and offered him naughty favours.
I offered him doughnuts of various flavours.
I cried and begged and got on my knees,
He looked at me angrily and said, 'Oh please!'

He pulled out a ticket, fined me forty pound,
I sobbed and banged my fist on the ground.
But I was at last, I was a criminal and not a good boy anymore,
So I stayed there with those pesky coppers,
Whimpering on the floor.

Tauseef Amjad (13)
Cranbrook College

THE EAGLE

There was once an eagle that flew,
Through the grey cloud and mist-hung skies,
Brown wings stretched out,
The eagle glides.

Watching the rattling and rumbling of the leaves,
Brown wings long and flexed,
The eagle flies.

Into the emerald deep,
Where the tree life thrives,
With the sharp, short beak open
The eagle dives.

On a plausible branch where the calm breeze creeps
With a bright green moon shining,
The eagle sleeps.

Above the rumbling and rattling leaves,
Making whistling noises,
High in the silent, speechless, bright blue sky
The eagle makes its home.

There was once a brown book
That described the brown eagle's life.

Dhruv Patel (12)
Cranbrook College

SWEET JAMAICA

I touch down from the plane,
Excited about my stay,
I smell the warm, moist air
On the outskirts of Montego Bay.

I settle down, atmosphere tame,
As I munch on my sweet chunk of sugar cane,
Until I join in Kingston's carnival parade
And dance till the morning of the next day.

That morning town's fast asleep,
I hear noises in the distance far away,
I've come to the beginning of another day.

This is Jamaica,
Where there are always things to see,
You can sit by watching the sea wave about,
In the shade of a coconut tree.

Jayson Mcleod (13)
Cranbrook College

THE FLIGHT

They soared so very high
Up in the dark, starry sky,
They looked down through their clear blue eyes
And one swooped down with a cry.

It caught a little blackbird sitting in its nest
And then flew back far above the rest,
And started to chew and swallow
With no doubts or sorrow.

All of a sudden the ground began to shake
The archaeopteryx was now awake,
So every creature went and hid in haste
For they knew if they stayed they'd be waste.

The archaeopteryx looked very big and bony
But if you felt it you'd realise it was very stony,
It would crush anything that stood in its path
And stroll away with a loud cruel laugh.

Jerome Heron (13)
Cranbrook College

THE GOOD SAMARITAN

As I was going to Jericho,
My heart was pounding.
I saw shadows of men
Who had come to give me a beating.
As I lay half dead
I thought I saw a priest in my head.
I know he saw me,
But left very quickly!
When the levite came,
I didn't think he would be the same.
But he knelt by me briefly,
Only to soon leave me.
So, when the Samaritan came
I assumed it would be the same!
However, he knelt and took care of my wounds
Took me to an inn and paid to keep me in.

Jack Allman (12)
Cranbrook College

LIFE

Life is what we live
Life is short
Life is hard
Life has bad parts
Life has good parts
Life is boring
Life is interesting
Life has surprising events
Life has a quick year
Life has quick and slow seconds
Life is fascinating
Life is too much studying
Life is too much knowledge
Life has little play
Life has more anger
Life has more happiness.

Joshua Wariebi (12)
Cranbrook College

CITIES LIKE LONDON

A gigantic city like London,
Growing as we are letting it be,
Six million people habitat in it,
Living in one of the many boroughs like me.
As I approach a crowd of people in Oxford Street
I feel the atmosphere of people hitting me.
When Buckingham Palace emerges from Admiralty Arch,
A reaction of amazement strikes me.
A city like London is indescribable,
Just like New York and Sydney.

Michael Myint (14)
Cranbrook College

Symphony In White

I had a dream last night,
About a world in white
There were stars that shone bright
Setting the black sky alight

I look up to see Arctic owls in flight
Soaring around at a great height
Causing mice to scatter in fright
Unwilling to ease the owls' hungry plight

White fluffy snow everywhere in sight
Sheep shivering in the face of Nature's might
Paws and noses suffering from frostbite
Who knows if they will live until morning light?

Sahal Quazi (12)
Cranbrook College

Winter

In the mid mist of winter,
The cold, icy wind is so bitter,
The months of January, February and December.
The ground covered in the thick and lush layer of snow,
Laid out like white turf all in rows,
Having snow fights with your foes
All the car windows are frosty
And the lakes all so icy
With the weather all so intensely chilly
December is now here, Christmas is near,
So get ready for presents, soft drinks and beer,
So enjoy as the festive spirits will be everywhere.

Ajay Bhaskaran (13)
Cranbrook College

Dream To Fly

I sit and look at the blue sky
And dream of flying thousands of feet high.
To be surrounded by white, fluffy clouds,
Instead of being crushed by large crowds.

To have wings just like a golden eagle,
Soaring high above all those busy people.
It is so tranquil with the wind in my face
The white and blue heavens is such a peaceful place.

But it is all a dream, my creative imagination,
A thought that gives me so much exhilaration.
One day I might just get the real feeling,
But until then I'll just keep on dreaming.

Luchien Anderson (13)
Cranbrook College

Firework Night

The sky filled with sparks and flames,
The children rush about.
Their cries are hardly heard
Jumping jacks and rockets are ever seen.

Dogs howl and cats cry
Frightened of the noise.
The sky is filled with cordite smoke.
The decorations are in the sky
Flashes here and there.

Because of all this noise nobody hears
A small little boy
Who is feeling pain.

Ibrahim Ahmed (14)
Cranbrook College

The Battle At Rugal Gate

In ancient, savage China
An epic battle took place,
Between the oppressive Zuhan empire
And the primitive yellow turbans.

The Zuhan empire was huge
And very efficient women,
They were organised, tactful and skilled
And ruled over the South of China.

The yellow turbans were fierce and war-like
And rebelled against the Zuhan, simple,
They were small in numbers and used weapons,
But they had heart, and that's what counted.

The stage was set for a historical battle,
It was battle at Rugal Gate,
Here held many a bloody war
And was sure to be epic.

As soon as the battle had started
You could see the turbans out-numbered,
But they were fighting as hard as they could,
They battled on with true vengeance, killing many opponents.

The Zuhan were looking like the favourites,
With their double-edged swords and battle axes
But the turbans were not giving up just then
Giving the Zuhan a run for their money.

When the bodies were cleared and the blood was spilled,
The Zuhan emerged victorious,
But the surviving turbans can come back knowing
That they gave it everything they could, at Rugal Gate.

Tisaru Perera (12)
Cranbrook College

FEELINGS DURING DEATH, IS THIS DEATH?

Thorny tree,
Forcing up my food pipe.
It feels terrible.
Is this death?

Things darkening,
Soon to pitch-black.
It's very scary.
Is this death?

Starting to remember,
The loved ones.
Feeling unhappy.
Is this death?

Thinking if
I can be cured.
Clueless
Is this death?

God,
I'm coming back.
Heaven or Hell,
It's your choice.

I don't want to die!
Thorny tree,
Has been released.
I see my body lay,
Doctors all around.
Death cannot be cured!
This is death!
Don't be afraid.

Asim Bhuta (14)
Cranbrook College

LIFE

One day I'll be free,
Free from sorrow, free from pain,
Free from anger, free from hate,
For on judgement day I'll know my fate.

Hell or Heaven,
Happy or sad,
A perfect life you'll never have.
Why grieve over death?

Why not rejoice?
Do not the dead go to a better place
After all?
People cry.

Children die,
The earth is rotting,
Yet we pretend it's all right,
We have our laughs.

This should make us feel better
Should it not?
Why do we love our lives so much,
It's only a venue for pain, agony and destruction?

We all are doers of evil one time or another,
So why even bother?
When I leave this earth I'll be glad
Glad for a life I never had.

Or will I cry in death,
Cry for what I've left behind?
A loving family, caring friends
Things that are sublime.

Jaimin Patel (11)
Cranbrook College

The City Of The Damned

On the breeze, the faint echo of your voice,
Your name is at the tip of my tongue,
My thoughts are dominated by your face,
The pain you have caused has bounded me here
In the City of the Damned.

Observing up and down the deep, black sky,
My past, my pain is written in the stars,
But they won't shine for me,
They won't guide me out of my darkness,
Lost

It's a carious wasteland, death's backyard,
His stench overcomes all other senses,
But life exists, lost souls searching for an exit,
Although my sight isn't failing,
Reality tells me they are deceiving me,

I have created an ocean with my tears,
I'm confused, I shouldn't be here,
But you've destroyed my sanity,
All alone to pick up the pieces,
With my bloodstained hands

Demons have released, they're torturing me,
Preparing me like a main course,
Tenderising my soul, ready for breakdown,
I'm powerless to them, they're ignoring my screams,
They will only answer to you

My eyes have dried, like an empty well,
I cannot fight anymore
I'm waiting for you
In the City of the Damned
My home . . . .

Simon Brindley (16)
Havering Sixth Form College

My Fun Life

I love my life
It's so much fun
I owe my thanks to my dad and mum.

My favourite time is at my sports
Football, swimming and karate.

I enter karate competitions regularly
And have many trophies
For the world to see.

I play football matches
With my friends, enjoying every minute
Right until the end.

Some we win, some we lose
But we try our best
So watch out for the blues.

Robert Clark (11)
Sanders Draper School

Gun

In my gun there is a golden bullet,
Opposite my gun there is a blown off head,
On my gun there is some blood.
My gun is inside my hand,
On my gun there is a trigger,
Beside my gun there are dead men.

Sebastian Massart (11)
Sanders Draper School

TERROR

Fear itself could not describe a day that happened last year,
on September 11th.
The screams and shouts when the first plane hit the first tower.
It was horrible.

Then another plane hits the second tower
which happened a while after and then the people in the other tower
started to escape before it collapsed.

Everyone was terrified at the sight, people around the world
were devastated and wondered what would happen next.
Then their questions were answered.

The first tower that was hit started to collapse
and everyone went mad and started to run away.
This could not get any worse. It did.

A while later the second tower started to collapse
and dust was everywhere.
After the dust settled a pile of rubble was left there.

A year on and we still remember that terrible day.

Rebecca Warren (11)
Sanders Draper School

THE BOX

Inside my box are many colours,
On my box there is a lid,
Under the box is a surface,
Opposite the box is a mirror,
Next to the box is a life,
Outside the box is a world.

Ameer Nasir (11)
Sanders Draper School

I Am A Washing Machine

I am a washing machine,
I live in a conservatory,
Under the table top.
I'm filled to the top,
With soapy water and clothes.
I wish I was alive,
Just for one day.
I smell of stinky socks and dirt I'd say.
In my belly
Where the clothes go in,
It spins so much, that I feel dizzy.
Where's my money. Oh no!
I don't have any.
When I'm working and getting wet.
What is that I see?
More clothes.
Now I have so much to do,
I'd better get going so see you soon!

Reema Chandni Unnadkat (12)
Sanders Draper School

I Am A Fridge

I am a towering, shiny refrigerating machine
I'm always so cold and I'm big and bold
I like the food they put in me, chocolate, jelly and stuff
But some food is smelly and muffed
I never move an inch, I'm always in the same place
On top of the freezer, my mate
I am always being opened, morning, afternoon and night
For breakfast, lunch and dinner, it's always a delight.

Jack Bruce (12)
Sanders Draper School

THE STORM

It was a cold and frosty morning,
Then suddenly the sky let out a warning,
In the corner of my eye there was a flash of lightning,
The sight was pretty frightening,
All of the shocked children ran into their house,
And patiently waited for the storm to stop
Like a little quiet mouse.
Rapidly the sleet and snow came pouring down
And then just laid there on the ground,
The children couldn't believe their eyes,
But then the storm went slowly,
Cautiously and died.

Stephanie Driscoll (12)
Sanders Draper School

THE BUS

Inside the bus there are people talking quietly,
People reading a paper and people on phones.
Outside the bus there are trees in the wind,
They sway from side to side.

Inside the bus there are men talking about the football,
'What a goal! What was he doing?' and 'Stupid ref!'
Outside the bus there are houses standing there looking in,
Waiting for their pets to come home.

Inside the bus the people look out,
Outside the people look in.

Michael Chaplin (11)
Sanders Draper School

My Cat

I had a small black cat
Who the vet said was too fat
So we cut down on his food
Which greatly altered his mood

He liked to scratch and bite
He did this with all his might
He'd hide behind a bush and pounce
And all the local cats he'll trounce

He liked to play with my woolly socks
But always ran away when he saw a big fox
He used to rip my lovely tights
But liked to stay out on stormy nights

He'd purr so loud he'd shake the house
But was very good at catching a mouse
He really was as mean as mean could be
If you're super brave do come and see.

Natalie Spilsbury (12)
Sanders Draper School

Flowers

F is for funky forget-me-nots
L is for lovely lilies
O is for orange marigolds
W is for winter snowdrops
E is for exciting elderflower
R is for red roses
S is for summertime sunflowers.

Elizabeth Boyle (12)
Sanders Draper School

Cats

You look out of your window in the morning
and the first thing you see is cats,
lots of different coloured cats,
some black, some white, some tabby and some tortoise ones
and they are all doing different things,
some gulping down food as if they haven't eaten in days,
others are preening, looking so elegant,
lots are sleeping in corners all curled up together,
some stalking a bird they look like tigers,
then, all of a sudden, a dog barks - they all freeze,
then, they all run,
now there are no cats eating, no cats preening, no cats sleeping
and no cats stalking,
until the morning when the park will be full again.
I'll get up especially - I think it's fun!

Jennifer Phelan (12)
Sanders Draper School

New Year's Eve

Gathered at my auntie's house,
Bottles of champagne popping like gunshots,
Everyone was laughing like hyenas.
At midnight the clock chimed like Big Ben.

Then there were fireworks, rockets,
Screaming like little babies and sparklers glittering like diamonds,
Party poppers streaming all the colours of the rainbow.
All around me people were cheering like a football crowd.

There was a table of food that looked like a feast fit for a king.
Everyone tucked in, they looked like vultures.
At the end they all went very silent, like a graveyard.

Samantha Holt (11)
Sanders Draper School

HAEMOLOVIN' YOU!

To my lover,
Through the Vena Cava,
You have stolen my heart,
Blood races through me like a dart,
Thanks to the high pressure,
I love you no lesser,
This is so true,
I'm Haemolovin' you!

The blood is pumped in,
Just to see you again,
For without any blood,
I'd be dud,
For you are my life's bain,
I need you as much as my pulmonary vein,
This is so true,
I'm haemolovin' you!

For the thing I've been talking (about),
The pigment haemoglobin,
It grabs onto oxygen,
So I can carry on loving,
The mountain of your approval I clamber,
It's like scaling the atrium chamber,
This is so true,
I'm haemolovin' you!

If I had 8 arms I'd cuddle you with all my tentacles,
It's nicer than being in the chamber of the ventricle,
By buying you chocolates I'd be doing things by halves,
To keep my heart pumping I need all the valves,
The one that I love you are the sorta',
If only I was as muscular as the aorta,
This is so true, I'm haemolovin' you.

William Morris (14)
Sanders Draper School

The Old Abandoned House

I walked into the old abandoned house,
it's now the oldest and scariest house in LA
I went in, the huge, old, rusty door
slammed shut behind me.

There was darkness
I heard loud footsteps, then a *crash*
I was feeling very scared now
the large oak door
squeaked like a mouse
When I opened it
I slowly and carefully
glanced around the room,
I began to walk in,
the room was large
and full of dust,
I walked over
to the old, red
and shabby curtains.
I opened them.

There was light

I heard another loud
bang from upstairs . . .

Then some more footsteps,
coming towards me . . .
I saw a shadow
I was so terrified
I saw a large, dark figure,
I tried to scream, but I couldn't . . .
then . . .
there was darkness.

Charlotte Russell (12)
Sanders Draper School

THE BULLDOZER

Smash! Crash! Bash!
As I destroy this house
I use my ball
I toot my horn
Then the house comes falling down!

I work and make a lot of noises
Demolishing buildings and bringing down houses!
Dust clouds all around me
Charging like a raging bull!
Smash! Crash! Bash!

I dream about blowing skyscrapers away,
But because they use bombs
I can only dream away.
I hate bombs, their *bangs* and *kabooms*
But I'm rock solid and I go *brrrmmm*
Whilst going
Smash! Crash! Bash!

Daniel Jones (12)
Sanders Draper School

DREAM

Inside my dreams is a paradise world
Throughout my dreams floats endless colours
Inside my dreams are my deepest secrets
Outside my dreams there is a reality
In the reality none of this is real.

Melissa Knight (11)
Sanders Draper School

THE STRAY CAT

The stray cat looks in through the window,
Watching the flames burning bright,
He longs to be loved and cared for,
He longs for a summer sight.

The cold winds through his legs,
As he curls up on the edge of the road,
He waits for a door to open
And a voice ushering him out of the cold.

It's been so long since his lips touched food,
It's been so long since a hand stroked his back,
Now he's settled down in a dustbin,
Resting in peace in a sack.

Lenita Rankin (12)
Sanders Draper School

UNDER THE SEA

Under the sea, fish move daintily as they play hide-and-seek
in and out of the coral.
Up on land, children play as they make their way to school.
Under the sea, an octopus scares all the little fish away
because he is so huge.
Up on land, you can hear little children crying,
adults shouting.
Under the sea, there are lots of sparkling flashing colours
of the little fish.
Up on land, there are new people being brought
into the world every day.

Jade Allen (11)
Sanders Draper School

FOOTBALL SUNDAY

It's Sunday morning yet again,
The football season has only begun,
The goals are up,
Who'll win the cup?

Both teams are steady,
As they get ready,
Before we knew it
They were in the kit.

We scored a goal,
It hit the pole,
They kicked off again,
They nearly did the same.

It was half-time,
The subs came off the line,
45 minutes left to go,
It seemed to go very slow.

We tried really hard,
But we got a red card,
They took a free kick,
Which was saved by Mick.

The whistle blew,
We all knew,
Amongst the rest,
We were the best!

Stephanie Randleson (11)
Sanders Draper School

I Am A Washing Machine

I am a washing machine,
I get used every day.
I am full of dirty underwear,
I am sure that is all I can say.
I am always getting turned on,
I am always getting turned off.
I am stuck under the bench, white and square,
I am always tasting dirt, dust and hair.

I turn the washing,
I turn it clean.
I am very loud, *click, clang, bang,*
I smell a lot of dirty socks, yuck!
I have wet, cold, dirty, smelly hands put stuff in my belly,
I then have cold hands getting the clothes out of my belly.
I have mums put screaming children in front of me,
I hear them cry every time I turn off.

I sometimes wish I were in the loft,
I wish I were on my own getting some sleep.
I am now getting old,
I am now getting slow.
I am now being put in a van,
I think I am going to the dump.
I see washing machines which have rusted away,
I think to myself I will look like that one day.

Laura Dennis (12)
Sanders Draper School

FIREWORK NIGHT

The fireworks were as loud as gun shots,
People oohed and arghed as the flame disappeared into thin air.
The bottles of champagne popped like popcorn in a hot pan.
The moonlight shone like a forest on fire,
The food was picked up like a mountain of gold.

It was as bright as a lighthouse light,
Guy Fawkes burned like a forbidden forest,
Wrappers from fireworks were gathered everywhere,
Party poppers popped like chewing gum.

When everyone went home the house was as quiet as a library,
Parents made us clean up with bribery,
Time's going fast like an Olympic race
We went to bed and fell asleep in our sheets of lace.

Sasha Tyler (11)
Sanders Draper School

HALLOWE'EN

Hallowe'en happens every year,
People dress up scary.
Witches on broomsticks
Wizards with wands
Gorillas look really hairy!

Do you want trick or treat?
Handing out sweets all night,
Creeping, screeching,
Bats and cats,
Really give you a fright!

Charlotte Watts (11)
Sanders Draper School

The Park

Next to the park is a busy road.
Inside the park there are loads of children.
Beside me are boys playing football.
Under me is some blood where somebody fell over.
Across the park are some trees dangling over the swings.
Opposite me is a squirrel eating a nut under the slide.
Below me are some sweet wrappers.
Above me is the sun shining down.

Thomas Pockett (11)
Sanders Draper School

The Train Ride

Outside the train we leave hundreds of trees behind.
In the train you can hear the train's wheels going over the tracks.
Above the train the clouds go whizzing past.
Next to the train we pass crowded stations.
Under the train there are rats scattering around.
Across the train I hear children's screaming and babies crying.
Outside the train it comes to a halt.

Michaela Wilson (12)
Sanders Draper School

The Fire

It started with a little flame,
Spreading billowing smoke,
A person in the upstairs room,
Soon began to choke.

He rushed to the nearest window,
The flames crackling and popping,
Oh help me, please help,
With the flame dancing and flopping.

Danielle Young (11)
Sanders Draper School

TORNADO

Tornado twists terribly,
Tearing trees up from the ground.
Trying to trick terrified children with its terrifying sound,
It was performing a destructive ballet.
It circled overhead, across the ground,
As if it was a sniffing bloodhound.
Swiftly it was gone destructively down the valley.

James Melrose (11)
Sanders Draper School

MY BROTHER

I banged a nail, it hit my thumb!
My brother laughed but my mum
Then my brother painted a big picture
But the problem was, it looked like a teacher
My brother then started to cry
My mother laughed and so did I.

Michael Titmus (12)
Sanders Draper School

Hallowe'en

Hallowe'en is as scary as Kat Slater with no make-up
Children like little mice scurrying from house to house
Lots of people having the living daylights scared out of them
By children with creepy costumes

Doors being slammed as if a sumo wrestler had done it
Dogs howling as if they have just been shot
Excited kids screaming and hollering
It seems as if there are volcanoes waiting to erupt
Angry adults fuming as they open their front door
To see who has been pranking them

As Hallowe'en draws to a close
For many children this is a night to remember!

Chukuma (Chuck) Pratt (11)
Sanders Draper School

The Garden

Inside the garden the pets live.
On the trees dark fruit grows.
Next to the trees the pond shivers.
On the pond the eggshells float.
Under the waterfall the secret cave is,
On the cave the green plants grow,.
Next to the plants is a small mountain,
On a mountain rock a worn-out pan lies.
Across from the pan is a field of grass,
On the grass the door shows you out of the garden.

Dean Williams (12)
Sanders Draper School

I Am A Washing Machine

I am a washing machine
I wash your socks
I wash your trousers
I wash your frocks
I work every day
I can't stop
I have no time to play
I am square
I hate that Calgon stuff
I think it tastes of bitter pear
I'd rather have Daz
I think it is faz
I'm endlessly feeling dizzy
I feel like having something fizzy
I'm always in for repair
I think it's a shame they just don't care.

Simon Weinand (12)
Sanders Draper School

Bonfire Night

The lights in the streets were as dim as can be,
Bangs were heard from all around,
Everywhere, there were lots of air coming from the mouths of people,
The bangs from the fireworks were louder than a lion's roar,
All lights were turned off, it was like being in the darkest of dark holes
Until the rocket went off in the sky,
It lit up the faces and my eye,
Some people were amazed, there were smiles on their faces,
As happy as can be,
Some people couldn't see in their eye
Because of the bright light in the sky.

Katy Stallan (11)
Sanders Draper School

My Thoughts

When I lay in bed thoughts go through my head
I think and I wonder
What I'll be when I'm older.
Will I be in a premier or scavenging
Through a dumpster,
But what I know for sure I can always turn to my mum's door.

When I lay in bed thoughts go through my head
I think and I wonder
What I'll be when I'm older.
Will I be a father with many mouths to feed
Or will I be a bachelor looking after my own needs.

When I lay in bed thoughts go through my head
I think and I wonder
What I'll be when I'm older.
Will I be a pop star chasing for number one
Or will I be a robber, always on the run.

When I lay in bed and these thoughts go through my head
I just . . . go . . . to . . . zzzzzzz.

Frank Rex (12)
Sanders Draper School

I Am A Washing Machine

I am a washing machine,
I love to make things clean.
I like it when they put clothes in my belly.
I see the babies watch me like a telly.
I am glad I am a washing machine.

Daniel O'Neill (12)
Sanders Draper School

I Am A Washing Machine

I am a washing machine full of dirty clothes.
I am a washing machine that everybody knows.
I am a washing machine, I hate working all day.
I am a washing machine but what can I say.
I am a washing machine, I've just broken down.
I am a washing machine, I sound like a clown.
I am a washing machine, the repairman has just come.
I am a washing machine, he's got a builder's bum.
I am a washing machine spinning round all day.
I am a washing machine washing the dirt away.
I am a washing machine tackling dirt, juice and tea.
I am a washing machine, what would life be like without me?

Jack Wilkinson (12)
Sanders Draper School

Bonfire Night

The bonfire crackled like popcorn,
It spat fire like a camel,
Blending colours like a palette of paint,
The smell of smoke filling our noses.

Fireworks bang louder than a gunshot,
The patterns explode like a volcano,
The colours looked like a splattered window,
They were as loud as a lion's roar.

Then they were gone!
As quick as a flash.

Chelsea Richardson (11)
Sanders Draper School

A Night To Remember

This day has a story which all can tell,
his name was Guy Fawkes,
who came with a promise
to blow up Big Ben.
His plot was foiled, what a relief
and that's what began this night of belief.

Families gather by fires,
at home and in parks,
to watch the night skies
come alive with dancing bright lights,
fireworks go *bang, whoosh* and scream,
we marvel at the sight for all to be seen.

Lewis Harrison (11)
Sanders Draper School

I Am A Popcorn Maker

I am a popcorn maker who loves people
to get excited about my popcorn
which tastes so nice and buttery inside their mouths.
I love it when the family sit down to watch a film
whilst eating what I make.
I love the smell of butter and toffee
it shows me that I'm loved.
I like to hear the noise I make
when my buttons are pushed.
I like to touch the new popcorn
from the popcorn box before I make it sweet.

Paul Kelley (12)
Sanders Draper School

The Blazing Fire

It started with a little flame,
Spreading, billowing smoke.
A person in the upstairs room,
Soon began to choke.

The person began to panic,
As the flames danced to her room.
The smoke crept to the ceiling
And she felt a sense of doom.

The fire crept beneath the door,
Flickering with all its might.
The little girl not feeling brave
Hid her eyes from the sight.

Sirens were heard all through the street,
As men tried to get ahead.
They got into the house too late,
The girl was already dead.

Nikki Eves (12)
Sanders Draper School

All In My Head

Under the bed lie creatures of fear
With big, scary fangs - or so I hear
Although my mum scares them away every night
They still give me a right old fright
But since they're just all in my head
I'll hide under the cover and pretend they're dead.

Callum Pearman (11)
Sanders Draper School

ABOVE AND BELOW

Opposite my bed sits my mum staring,
Under my bed sits a monster glaring,
On top of my bed lies me asleep,
Dreaming happily and then, *beep, beep.*

Opposite my house is a red bus,
My mum needs to clean because there's lots of dust,
Under my house are lots of pipes,
On my house are Christmas lights.

Up in the sky are twinkling stars,
Underneath are lots of cars,
I wonder what's above the sky,
Everyone says Heaven is, when we die.

Daniel Ridley (11)
Sanders Draper School

IN THE BOX

In the box I shall put
The tears of death,
The cries of people in need of aid
And the pain of owners beating their pets.

In the box I shall put
Bloody wars,
Suffering, hate, greed
And best of all I will put Satan himself in there,
With the fiery pits of Hell.

I will lock the box and throw away the key,
Now I have made the world a better place to live in . . .

Samantha Barnes (11)
Sanders Draper School

A Heart

There sat a heart,
All on its own,
With none of its friends,
It's alone, it's alone.

But then he saw it,
With a glimpse of a look,
That was it,
He was took, he was took.

He stared at it madly,
He had never felt so good,
Then he walked over to it,
Just the way he should.

What a beautiful lady,
She's so lovely,
She looks all alone,
Do you think she's for me?

Zachary Chouman (11)
Sanders Draper School

Hallowe'en

Along the streets on the night of Hallowe'en
It's as dark as a black cat,
Then you see little children,
As scary as a raging herd and as happy as clowns.
Then you get pumpkins turning to jack-o'-lanterns.
While they were like large fireballs,
Decorations like a tiger,
Fierce and thoughtless, bold and brighter.

Nicky Wells (11)
Sanders Draper School

I Am A Dishwasher

I am on when no one is around
and filled with more things everyday.
I am loved and used by the whole family
(so they don't have to wash up).
I love what my owner leaves me to eat up,
especially with soap and water.
I am a dishwasher, I love to wash,
I live for washing, I worship washing.
I graduated from washing school in the year 1999.
I have had other jobs,
I have been a washing machine,
a tumbler and a fridge.
I get people to look in me when I am ill
and I make an awful racket.
I am a dishwasher.
I go to all the parties.
I'm under the kitchen sink.

Matthew Haywood (12)
Sanders Draper School

The House

The house that you could see for miles,
There was a man on the roof fixing tiles,
The door creaked and fell,
Outside there was a well,
Inside there was a painting on a wall,
It looked like it was about to fall,
Eeek! What was that?
Phew! It was only the cat!

Maria Dunn (12)
Sanders Draper School

I Am A Washing Machine

I am a washing machine,
I am square and a brilliant colour of white,
I have a beautiful belly that is opaque,
I clean tonnes and tonnes of stained and sweaty clothing,
I live in a big bright kitchen
underneath the worktop, next to the warm tumble dryer.
I spin fast and furious like a car wheel going at max speed.

I use lovely frequencies that make the clothes
smell fresh throughout the day,
I have loads of buttons, which make me turn on or off,
I have little creatures watching me at my job,
I work every single hour of the day but I enjoy it,
I use bundles of water to make the clothes clean.

Josh Oakley (12)
Sanders Draper School

I Spy

I spy with my little eye a room filled with gold and blue.
This room is for everyone, even including you!

I smell with my little nose drafts of all many spices.
I also smell pepper, probably cut into slices.

I hear with my little ear sizzling from a pan.
I hear a lot of rushing, I also hear my nan.

I taste with my ticklish tongue chicken filled with spices and curry.
It's burning my tongue now so I better hurry!

I feel with my handy hands lots of doors and a sink.
I finished my poem now so you'd better think!

Sam O'Vens (12)
Sanders Draper School

I Am A Washing Machine

I am a washing machine,
white and rectangular with a window
under the cupboard all day
waiting for some clothes to be cleaned every day.
I am being switched on and off
every day my buttons are wearing away.

I spin very fast,
I'm feeling dizzy and clean the clothes very fast.
I hate washing my dad's socks
because they smell of rotten boots.
I will need a gallon of powder
to get them smelling like powder.

I've got two spins, one extra fast and dizzy
when I look at the glass,
I'm pleased when I get to the end of the spin,
I hope they don't use me soon again.
I know it won't be long before I get a headache again.

I spin around so fast I make loud noises
like Michael Schumacher driving so fast.
I hate the noise I make because it makes me shake.

Scott Tungatt (12)
Sanders Draper School

What's Under The Bed?

Under the bed there are all kinds of things,
horrible, disgusting things
big monsters waiting to grab you
rats nibble at your bed
beetles crawling up to you
insects scuttling around.

Under the bed there are all kinds of things,
nice things
old Christmas presents
your Game Boy
your favourite game
old teddies you got when you were two.

Marianna Alexandrou (11)
Sanders Draper School

Squirrels

Here I listen to the morning birds
Sitting quietly writing these words,
Cars in the distance driving by
I take a big stretch and then a big sigh.

Watching the squirrels jump from tree to tree
I sit waiting, hoping they'll come to me,
My hand is held out with a palm full of bits
One climbs down a branch and there it sits.

Eyes are upon me, watching me glance
It can't decide whether to take the chance,
The gap gets smaller between it and me
It then gets the courage and comes for the feed.

The wait is all over, I sit back and smile
The squirrel goes off and disappears for a while,
I then spot it burying the food in the ground
There it'll be back when no one's around.

Chantelle Carter (11)
Sanders Draper School

HALLOWE'EN

It's Hallowe'en,
It's time to scare,
Witches flying through the air.
Black cats hissing,
Having fun,
The long dark night has just begun.

Children screaming with delight,
All this happens on one scary night.
Trick or treaters,
Knocking on doors
Collecting candy,
The kind they wished for.

The big shining moon,
Lights up the night sky,
The stars hide behind clouds,
It's as if they were shy.

Demons are hiding deep in the woods,
Keep an eye open,
They're after your goods.
It's Hallowe'en night so all beware,
Hope you're prepared,
You're up for a scare.

Grace Sussex (11)
Sanders Draper School

CAT HAIKU

I am calm and cute,
I'm white and brown with blue eyes,
I'm energetic.

Ashley Benningfield (12)
Sanders Draper School

I Am A Washing Machine

I am a washing machine,
I get used every day.
I regularly wonder why,
I never get paid.

I am always odorous,
I'm always full of socks,
I can't escape,
I hate those purple frocks.

I get switched off,
I get switched on,
I'm always working,
I'm always singing songs.

I hear their footsteps,
I see their shoes.
I feel their hands,
I get the blues.

I'm stuck in the kitchen,
I'm all on my own.
I'm always wishing
I can move home.

I get fed soap powder,
I think it's Daz.
I feel like a monster,
I feel like Taz.

I also get fed another soap,
Ariel I think,
They put it in me so
Their clothes don't stink.

Toni Watson (12)
Sanders Draper School

A Christmas Celebration

The frost falls as quick as a cheetah,
Its glistening sparkle was like a disco ball,
The sound of music filled the air like a raging storm,
The decorations were as pretty as a flower.
It was Christmas!

Children making snowman from the ice-cold snow,
The snow was as pale as Snow White's face,
The food was as hot as the sun.

The sound of children playing was as loud as a lion's roar
But nobody would say anything.
Everyone was laughing like a choir of hyenas being released
from the zoo.
The rhythm of the dancing was like the heartbeat of a sailor in a storm.
Christmas brings joy like a newborn opening its eyes.

Amy Munro (11)
Sanders Draper School

I Am A Teddy Bear

I am snugly and warm, hold me tight if there is a storm,
If you squeeze me too tight I will never put up a fight,
I'll keep you safe all through the night,
I will be your best friend for evermore,
I will never become a bore,
I am the perfect person to talk to,
I'll always listen to you,
If you ever have a problem,
I have the ideal shoulder to cry on,
I am always there for you.

Alicia Thompson (12)
Sanders Draper School

I'M A WASHING MACHINE

I'm a washing machine
I clean lots of smelly, dirty clothes
I have all these buttons
I spin extremely fast
I get filled with detergent.

I get faces looking in my stomach
I'm a big, white square shape
I'm always looking at piles of washing
Outside of my see-through stomach.

I live under a kitchen unit of my own
I am next to the dishwasher
I go around for about an hour
I really wish I got paid.

Jody Overington (12)
Sanders Draper School

THE WEDDING

She walked down the aisle,
The church full of fairy lights,
It was like a picture in a fairy tale,
Prince and princess in their castle.
At the party
The lights were flashing,
People were dancing,
People were laughing,
Time for the dance,
Their first dance as husband and wife,
Like a dream,
It was magic!

Victoria Coleman (11)
Sanders Draper School

Candy

I have a rabbit called Candy
Who likes all kinds of flowers especially pansies
But her favourite food of all is carrots and cabbage
She can be really good, but there's the odd times she's not.
She likes to chew the wood in her hutch
But most of all she likes chewing paper
My rabbit can be tidy or messy
But I don't care because she's my baby
When she's set free she rolls around in the mud
And has the time of her life
You would not think she likes cuddles and kisses
Because she does but whatever she does,
I know I'll always love her
And she will love me back.

Jade Clark (13)
Sanders Draper School

New Year

A long new year is here,
It's as long as a wise man's beard.
Fireworks go off at night
They're as loud as thunder and very light.
People line up along the street, moving their feet to the beat,
Singing songs loud like a bird.
The people indoors watch TV and count down from 33,
They sit as quiet as a worm, nice and peaceful, they don't squirm.
The whole country is celebrating,
Some loud, some quiet, like a pack of lions.
It all ends within a day,
Like someone's life, it drifts away.

Jake McGuinness (11)
Sanders Draper School

Betty's Birthday

My nan and grandad came round
I started to feel so proud
The cake was as big as a ball
The candles were a light.

I saw all the family singing
Oh, what a happy sight
It was like a dream come true for Betty
Seeing all her presents scattered about.

The party got going
And the lemonade was flowing
The party poppers came out
And with a big breath I shout,
'Happy birthday!
Happy birthday!
Happy birthday Sis!'

Rebecca Holman (11)
Sanders Draper School

Softly

Softly my brother tiptoes to bed
Softly the spider spins its web
Softly the trees rustle in the breeze
Softly my mum gets up with ease
Softly the milk's all lined up in rows
Softly the bird flies and crows
Softly my brother gets out of bed
Softly the spider respins its web.

Rio Caley (12)
Sanders Draper School

Hallowe'en

It's the 31st of October,
So what does that mean?
Trick or treating, witches, spooks
Why of course it's Hallowe'en.

Scary faces from pumpkins glow
Oooh what an eerie sight,
Cobwebs, bats, spiders everywhere
The children scream with fright.

Home at last, bags overflow
Look at all those treats,
Off to bed, hours later
Tummies full of sweets.

Over again for another year
Away go hats and cloaks,
Store them lovingly with care
For this time next year folks.

Kelsey Oates (11)
Sanders Draper School

A Celebration Of A Hair-Raising Hallowe'en

H allowe'en is as scary as Friday the 13th
A ll children are petrified like stone
L ollies to lick as big as your face
L aughter and screams as noisy as a coven of witches
O ut come werewolves as scary as my mum
W itches fly around like bats out of hell
E very boy and girl dressed up like monsters
E ach with a goody bag stuffed full like a turkey
N ow time for bed as snug as a bug in a rug.

Laura Pickess (11)
Sanders Draper School

Do I Remember That Day?

I don't know why it happened,
I don't know how it did,
I just seem to remember
My mouth turning black.

I felt it down my chin
I felt it in my throat
I felt it in my cheeks
I always hated black jacks.

My mum told my sister not to,
But she did it anyway,
She put that smelly black jack in my mouth,
Do I remember that day?

I started to cry
So my sister ran away,
She hid in the bathroom,
I remember that day.

Emma Matthews (11)
Sanders Draper School

Brown

Highlighted hair could be natural or man-made,
My elegant eyeshadow makes me feel boastful,
The printed pictures are exotic,
My practical pens are my favourite instrument for colouring
And of course do not forget my colourful carpet,
Which I feel privileged to stand on.

Elisabeth Mann (11)
Sanders Draper School

My New School

S mart uniform at our school,
A ssembly every Monday in the hall.
N ew students, old students all over the place,
D innertime comes - one big race.
E nglish, maths, science and PE
R ushing to each lesson gracefully.
S anders is the school for me.

D oing our homework by the deadline,
R eading, writing - all the time.
A chievements, credits we try to gain,
P ractising skills and using our brain.
E xercise books and bags to hold,
R emembering the things that we have been told.

Nadene Kennedy (11)
Sanders Draper School

Wedding Celebration

As scared as a squirrel,
He had a buzz like a bee,
Thinking about walking down the aisle,
Made him as excited as can be.

He felt as cold as ice,
As nervous as a cat,
When the wedding finally came,
He was sneaking around like a rat.

Saying, 'I do' was the happiest day of his life,
They were as happy as a daisy
And when he kissed his wife
They were as ecstatic as having their newborn baby.

Jamie Taylor (11)
Sanders Draper School

We Will Never Forget Them

The plane comes flying in,
Bang! the first tower is gone,
Then another plane comes flying in,
Boom! they are both gone!
They will always be in our minds,
We will not forget them.

The tears are trickling down my face,
As I hear the news,
The Twin Towers are gone.
Where, no one knows,
Deep down in the ground,
No one knows and no one will.

Anneka Fisher (11)
Sanders Draper School

The Great Storm Of Hatred And Jealousy

I always peer outside, beneath the gaps of the wooden door.
Seeing what lies behind the door of all wonder
I see the howl of the frightening wind blowing grey clouds.
Like a thunderstorm waiting to emerge
In front of me I see children
pulling their coats around them tightly as they shiver.
The horrible sight of parents
saying to their children, 'Hold on, don't let go.'
It breaks my heart to see families separating
all because of the great storm.
I wish to go and save them but I know
I would be the eye of the storm of hatred and jealousy.

Sarah Connor (11)
Sanders Draper School

Wedding Nerves

He was standing there, at the end of the aisle,
she hadn't yet turned up.
Like a lemon he stood not knowing what to do,
his nerves were raging like a mad driver on the run.
Where had she got to?

Do do do do . . . the organ started
and the flowergirl strode down the aisle like a princess
delivering rose petals as a path for the bride.

Like a swan the bride glided in a gown as white as snow.
The guests stared, the mothers cried and the groom stood
with eyes open wide, mouth open, looking like a goldfish.

By the time they knew it the rings were slipped on
the veil was lifted, a kiss was made and the party had started!

Amie O'Keefe (11)
Sanders Draper School

Rachel The Vampire

She walks in the night all on her own
'Blah, blah, blah Rachel,' she groans
Along comes Buffy the Vampire Slayer
And Rachel dissolves layer by layer.

As she dissolves along comes her brother Matt
With big, bushy, long hair like a cat
He saves poor Rachel from her internal hell
And that is the story that Rachel tells.

Calum Sharp (12)
Sanders Draper School

I'M A WASHING MACHINE

I am a huge white, shiny, clean washing machine.
My owner uses me 24/7.
Here she comes now with a basket full of dirty washing.
I have a window for my tummy.
She switches me on to wash
And pours a tasty liquid juice into my mouth.
I have cleaned the clothes and now I'm dizzy.
I am ready to do another wash but there is no washing.
I don't like the noise I make when I switch off.
Click, clog, click, clog, click, clog.

I'm ready now!
I'm getting very hungry again.

Lauran Lechmere (12)
Sanders Draper School

MY FACE

My face is round, my skin is fair
People say that's because I've got blonde hair
I have round eyes, they are dark blue
I don't wear glasses because I can see you!
My nose is long and quite thin
My glowing cheeks have dimples in!
I have long eyelashes, which are also fair
That's because they match my hair!
I have lots of freckles on my nose
In the summer they really show!
My ears are pointed like Dr Spock
There you are, that gave you a shock!

Rhys Battye (11)
William Edwards School

SUNDAY FOOTBALL

Sunday is a day to lay, lots of holy people pray.
But I go my own way, cos football's the game I like to play!

I put my boots on by the door, my mother's chin hits the floor.
She waits all day hoping I will score!

The whistle goes, the game begins, I hope my team
Adds another match to its wins!

Right from the start, I can hear my heart,
It's beating fast, I'll get the ball past!

I dribble the ball down the left hand side,
The other team gasp and one even cried!

They tackle me high, they tackle me low,
But only I know where I'm going to go!

I hit the ball, I hear my dad roar.
The ball goes in, *I score!*

Leaside are the winning team,
If you join them your face will beam!

That's how I like to spend my Sunday
And everyday including Monday!

Thomas Gilbank (11)
William Edwards School

DRUGS

Goodbye, I'm going through the door,
This stuff's always putting me on the floor.
Every time I have to take,
A piece of my life will break.
When I walk up on the cliff,

My legs become way too stiff.
Now I feel like I'm soaring,
Laying in the sea on a rainy morning
Now that I had got high
My life was taken so I had to die.

John Thompson (13)
William Edwards School

The Beach

The beach is great
I visited when I had just turned 8
The sand on your feet
And the waves lapping on top of it
Is like a picture you would love to have
The castles scattered everywhere
Step on them, you would not dare
The fish are caught and eaten
The wind blows against the coast.

The tide comes in
People can see a shark's fin
Panic hits all
Its jaws soaked with blood
Some men eventually slaughter it
And sell the meat for a high price.

Darkness falls
And people start to make fires
And cook food
In-between the rocks
Crabs are lurking
Waiting for scraps of food
That fall from our hands and mouths.

Daniel Gray (12)
William Edwards School

My Face Poem

Hair as stiff as rock, straight.
The blonde patches stand out
From the rest of the brown-coloured crowd.

Further down the oval structure,
The eyes, a mix of blue and green,
Skirmishing for the land.

The nose with its rounded base
Placed dead in the middle of the face,
Surrounded by the other features,
It breathes silently.

Further down, a wide but narrow gap,
Fills the space on the face . . . the mouth.
It comes in different structures,
Smiling, happy, dull or sad.

The face is yours to treasure
It cannot be changed.

Joe Pavitt (11)
William Edwards School

The Old Man's Death

Today is the day we celebrate the old man's death,
We remember his life and his very smelly breath.
He was a short old man, with freckles on his face
And he met a few friends as he went from place to place.
But there he lies now in a coffin all alone
Yet the crowds of people round him still smell his poor cologne.

Laura Sach (12)
William Edwards School

My Face Poem

My face isn't fat, skinny or too round,
it's not too oval like a rugby ball,
but it's my face only and my face forever.

My ears are big like a little elf,
but at least they're not hairy, waxy or pointy
but it's my face only and my face forever.

My hair is thick, heavy and long,
but it's not stringy, thin or fluffy,
but it's my face only and my face forever.

My eyes are green and blue,
they're quite big, but not really small and vainy,
but it's my face only and my face forever.

My lips are big, shaped and pinkish,
they're not too skinny or hairy,
but it's my face only and it's my face forever!

Kelly Broadbent (11)
William Edwards School

Face Poem

A rounded face like a ball,
Two endless pits of brown darkness,
A nose long as a straight ski slope,
Plump lips surrounding a deep red cave,
The grooves in the ears twist and turn like a racetrack,
Two hairy caterpillars crawl across the eyes,
Fields of brown barley across your head,
A smile bearing white jagged rocks.

Jacob Smith (11)
William Edwards School

HALLOWE'EN

First you get a pumpkin
And put a face on it.
Then we get our costumes
And wear them bit by bit.
Some people go as witches,
Some people go as ghosts.
Some people go as monsters,
They're what scare me most.
Then you go trick or treating,
People give you sweets.
When you have enough,
They make lovely treats.
Now Hallowe'en's nearly over
Your bags have filled their best
And all the ghouls and ghosts
Have now gone back to rest.

Colin Oakley (12)
William Edwards School

MYSELF

I hate my head,
I like my mind,
It's an everlasting wind.

I like my personality,
It stays with me all day,
It keeps keen and wanting to play.
I hate this body
Can't you see?
Sometimes I even don't want to be.

Thomas Wyborn (11)
William Edwards School

CELEBRATIONS

Celebrations, celebrations,
What lovely things,
Presents, gifts, prizes galore,
Celebrations are for all the important things in life,
Weddings, birthdays, Christmas and more.
New jobs and children,
Parties are thrown
Shouting, music, dancing galore.
Charity shows have parties for money,
To give to the poor and needy I think.
Everyone loves them,
People adore them.
Celebrations, celebrations,
There's more fun for all.

Adam Walters (12)
William Edwards School

DIWALI

This is the time of the year where you see candles,
We pray and pray till God is with us,
Bright light that enters every room.

This is the festival to celebrate light,
When we see the light, we are filled with joy,
We celebrate this festival so we can be free.

If I help others, I see bright light,
If I'm with greed, I see darkness,
Diwali, Diwali, Diwali.

Simeran Ghataora (12)
William Edwards School

My Face

My face may be oval, chubby or square
but it's mine and nobody elses.
My ears might be hairy, pointed or waxy
but they're mine and nobody elses.
My eyes might be beady, sparkling or brown
but they're mine and nobody elses.
My nose might be spotty, squashed or round
but it's mine and nobody elses.
My hair might be curly, stringly or I could be bald
but it's mine and nobody elses.
My mouth might be big, small or wide
but it's mine and nobody elses.
So when you look at me and if you don't like what you see
don't worry because it's my face and nobody elses.

Charlotte Hinton (12)
William Edwards School

World Cup

It's the main football event in four years,
The crowd's roaring with thundering cheers.
Last minute team talk in the changing room,
As fans wonder if it would be their team's doom.
Teams jog out onto the pitch,
As fans buy their last cheeseburger from McDonald's
A few yards from the pitch.
That's it, whistle blows,
Ball gets kicked, off it goes.
Chins drop to the floor,
'Come on England, will you score!'
Michael Owen's on the ball,
Wait a minute . . . it's a *goal!*

James Bell (12)
William Edwards School

Fun Run

Hip hip hooray! Here we go,
I hope I win, but I doubt it though
I'm on the starting line ready to run
When is the starter going to fire the gun.

I'm not in the lead but doing alright
It's all about finishing and I think I just might.

All those up front were born to run
But the rest of us are here just for some fun.

Everyone seems to find it funny
But I've just been overtaken by Bugs Bunny.

I finally finish, I'm over the line
Five and a half hours isn't a bad time.

I'm out with my family now to celebrate
I'm aching all over so I won't be out late.

Hayley Pulfer (11)
William Edwards School

Hallowe'en

H allowe'en is a time of year
A time for evil to roam the Earth
L eaving your homes to go trick or treating
L ongingly waiting for that day to arrive
O h, what joy to scare your worst neighbours
W anting as much candy as you can possibly get!
E erie creatures flood the streets
E veryone with friends to meet
N othing is better than Hallowe'en!

Jade Barker (12)
William Edwards School

CHRISTMAS

Finally the day has come
Shops now closed
Churches bustling with families
Children itching to get home -
What has Santa got them?

Old relatives arrive
'Haven't you grown!'
'Aaah, she's so sweet!'
Later they settle for dinner -
Roast potatoes, stuffing, veg and gravy
Silence . . .

Once dinner's over
They all settle down -
Watching the EastEnders Christmas special.

12 midnight comes and goes
Everyone asleep
Children dreaming of their presents
Adults of their credit card bills!

Sarah Mitchell (12)
William Edwards School

BABY BOY

B abies are so precious
A nd are the future now
B ecause they're made from love
Y oung angels from above

B ecause God loved your child so
O h God did not let go
Y our day has surely come - you have a baby son.

Brooke Mason (12)
William Edwards School

MOVING

I move houses quite a lot
And every house has its own spot
Moving, moving, make new friends
All this moving shall never end

And every house has its own school
I have many first days to look like a fool
Re-decorating the house is always doom
But I never get my own room

The best thing about moving
That is so fun and not dooming
I always love a good house warming
But sometimes it could be boring

Best of all I like new house gifts
The jokes on the cards give you lifts
When it's all over they all go home
All the mess they made makes my mum moan.

Frank Attah (12)
William Edwards School

MY CHRISTMAS

C hristmas Day is finally here.
H ave we all let out a cheer?
R eindeer flying in the sky
I s that Father Christmas?
S now is falling on the ground,
T he family is gathering around.
M um is cooking Christmas pud
A nd Dad sleeps, if only he could. But . . .
S oon it will be time for the presents.

Crystal Gansbuhler (12)
William Edwards School

Siberian Tiger

S nowy white,
I mprints of
B lack lines,
E verlasting beauty,
R oaring, calling,
I dentifying his lonely feelings,
A nswers replying . . .
N one.

T igers come charging,
I solated by his family,
G ran, Mum, Dad, sisters and brothers,
E veryone here,
R oaring, calling no more.

Lauren Devereaux (13)
William Edwards School

Guess

I get up at 4 o'clock in the morning
And make a cup of tea.
Then I wake my brother and sister
So then is just us three.
We wake my mum and dad
And have a cup of tea
Then we go back downstairs
And turn the lights on the tree.
Then one by one we open our presents
Very joyfully.
Can you guess what my poem is about now?
It's very easy
It's about Christmas and my family.

Alexandrea Palmer (12)
William Edwards School

Footy Game

F ootball is a fabulous sport.
O ur whole world plays it.
O n the moon aliens play it as well.
T he world's favourite sport is footy
B oys and girls can play it
A nd even nans and grandads
L ob the keeper
L augh out loud

S tand back and watch the replay
T urn around, look at the crowd
A nd celebrate with your mates.
D efenders line up in the wall
I n the wall the defence stands tall
U pon the edge of the box
M otors are going in Beckham's head
As he lines up to take the kick
Soaring high, curling round the wall
Flying into the back of the net.

Christopher Webb (12)
William Edwards School

Roses Are Red

Roses are red
Violets are blue
Flowers are beautiful
And so are you
But I am wrong,
For you are more beautiful
Than a bird's song.

Antony Lane (12)
William Edwards School

SANTA - FIREWORKS

All animals are afraid of the noise
Children drop their favourite toys
Some fireworks are packed in big blocks
Some fire in coloured flocks.

The firework turned but then it burned
First it exploded, then it reloaded
They went of the wrong way,
Some hit Bombay.
I hit Big Ben as it struck 10
So remember, remember the 5th of November
When Big Ben struck 10
And then fell over.

Do you know who it was
No, not the Wizard of Oz
A man called Santa
Who likes orange Fanta
He drives a sleigh, don't crash I pray
During March, April and May.

Alex Douglas (12)
William Edwards School

POEM ON DRUGS

D rugs can kill a load of people
R eally! Just by taking one drug
they can make you become addicted to them
U sually if you try one and you don't like it you stop.
G reat you say, but if you are trying them, here's a little advice
S o, get your life sorted or they'll take over you
for the rest of your life!

Lesley Biggins (13)
William Edwards School

THE SUN

The sun's heat can
melt solid lead;
so say goodbye to
your feet or your head.

The sun can be used
to power our homes;
dishwashers, TVs
and our telephones.

The core of the sun
is about 20 million degrees;
I prefer a slight
gentle breeze.

After a while our
sun will disappear;
after that will have
everything to fear.

Craig Siddons (12)
William Edwards School

DRUGS

D isasters happen,
R eally high,
U sers die,
G one forever,
S erious consequences.

Phillip Whelpton (13)
William Edwards School

Ambush Blood

All hail tyrannus, the dinosaur lord
All who oppose us must die
The infiltration has begun.

Whispers in the night of a new found hero
A hero to save them all
Movements in the bushes, sleg troops tread cautious
Bang, bang, 2 men shot dead
With blood pouring from their heads
The silence continues
Then a war club thrown at a troop's head
The alarms are off, the armies are watching.

Now the most unexpected creature of them all
A spider let off a powerful gas to kill the armies
But streaking behind was a worker
Who shot the anonymous man
The battle is won
The world is doomed.

Ben Kelly (12)
William Edwards School

Drugs Poem

D rugs are bad
R uins your life
U sers losers
G ives you pains and problems
S o don't take drugs or you'll end up thugs.

Ellis Goldsmith (14)
William Edwards School

THE CELEBRATION

Sprayed snow windows,
Blazing fire,
Adding the final touches to the tree,
Putting out milk and cookies for Santa,
Pinning up the stocking on the mantel piece,
Waiting for Santa,
Off to bed to rest that sleepyhead.

Morning has risen,
Two flapping dressing gowns,
Running down the stairs,
Paper and bows falling to the floor,
As the two children unwrap some more,
Mum and Dad making coffee,
Children dancing round the room
With their presents.

Andrew Baker (12)
William Edwards School

GOD'S DINNER

The sea is the soup of God,
The crustaceans, little spices of flavour in the soup,
The boats, small spoons that stir the mixture.

The land is the food of God,
The humans, tiny cooks adjusting the food,
The vehicles, small knives and forks, preparing the food.

The swimming pools are the drink of God,
The inflatable toys, flavours of the cocktail,
All this makes God happy, to continue creating the world.

Rebecca Gray (13)
William Edwards School

RAIN

The rain drops on the window,
It slowly squirms side to side,
The thunder rumbles louder and louder,
As the dark skies get nearer and nearer to your position,
The raindrops pour on you like there's no tomorrow,
The raindrop still slowly squirms to the bottom of the window,
The lightning flashes quickly in the corner of your eye,
The thunder is still getting louder and louder,
The dark skies are nearly above you,
The lighting flashes faster and faster in your eyes,
You hope it doesn't come closer and closer to you,
The raindrops drop quicker and quicker,
But still that raindrop squirms down the window,
Now the raindrop has reached the bottom of the window,
The raindrop falls to the ground into a puddle
With the raindrops that went before it,
Now a new raindrop begins the journey.

Dilvinder Sander (12)
William Edwards School

DRUGS

Drugs make you high
they make you think that you can fly
whilst soaring high in the sky.
You imagine that your worst fears come to life
so then you commit suicide.
Your friends do drugs,
so if you want to wake up tomorrow
please, I beg of you, do not follow.

Billy Harvey (13)
William Edwards School

COMMONWEALTH GAMES

People come from East and West,
To see in sports, who's the best?
The celebration starts from here,
So do sit back and watch my dear.

People proud, waving their flag,
You won't see anyone reading a mag.
From football to continuous tennis,
You might see a streaker causing menace.

Athletes, striving for medals,
Cyclists, wearing out their pedals.
Divers jumping off the board,
Footballers celebrating when they've scored.

The gymnasts look smart, without a speck of dirt,
The netballers are racy, with their swishy skirts.
My favouritist sport is ping-pong,
But it gets boring when the volley's long.

In the end, we come together as one
And we should look back to what we've achieved and done.
We'll meet again in the next four years,
Who knows what will come when the future nears.

Seema Malvankar (13)
William Edwards School

THE PILL

D isasters lurk
R un down by a Merc
U nder the wheels
G one. No more pills!

Lee Buttner (13)
William Edwards School

Gory Story

Top of stairs.
Very scared.
Sniffing glue.
Head goes *zoom*
Everywhere.
Someone there
Saying, 'No',
But I'm gonna go.
Bumping down.
Round and round.
Great big sound.
Hit the ground.

Aaron Riley (13)
William Edwards School

Firework's Night

On the 5th of November
we celebrate fireworks night.
As they go bang the colours come out
they brighten the sky
and you hear a shout.
You can get quite pretty ones
or horrible loud ones
that make big bangs
and set off car alarms.
So remember
the 5th of November.

Chevelle Harwood (12)
William Edwards School

My World

A world where I can be me
A world where nobody can see

This is my world with my rules
A world with theme parks and pools

A world with good people not bad
A world where no one feels sad

A world where you can do as you please
A world with perfect trees with perfect leaves

A world where you're part of a team
This world, my world is my dream.

Jenna Yeomans (12)
William Edwards School

The Sea

Waves lapping on the beach,
down into the deep abyss,
nothing down there but emptiness.
Then *swish!* little fish
little shoals of fish everywhere
big fish are also there.
Sitting and waiting . . .
then *swipe!* Dinner time! Yum!

Elizabeth Colledge (12)
William Edwards School

My Weekend At Portsmouth

My weekend at Portsmouth,
It was very hard.
Ten hours drill a day,
Marching, shouting, balling, screaming.
Emotions running riot, being away from home,
Even though it was hard, I still got through.
Sleeping was horrible in the itchy bunks upon the ship,
HMS Bristol, the type 42 destroyer.
This weekend made me think,
Do I still want to be in the navy?
Should I still be a sea cadet?
Yes!

Chris Beven (12)
William Edwards School

Drugs

Drugs are the things that make you high
You think you're flying with the birds in the sky
You see things that are not always there
Some little things might give you a scare
Dogs, fish, birds or cats
Be out too late and get eaten by gnats
You get scared and go somewhere high
You jump off the edge, get ready to die.

Louis Hawker (13)
William Edwards School

Drug Poem

Do you know the dangers,
That wait around the corner?
First you try it as a joke,
Then you take it like it's Coke.

Then friends stay away
And family too,
As you get aggressive
And unfair too.

You don't have much money
But need it for drugs
So you get involved in crime
And can't find a way out.
Your life light is fading
And you're acting very weird
You collapse on the floor.

One year later you're underground
And you are not happy with what you found.

If only you had listened to what everyone said,
Then you would not be dead.

Don't make this mistake, as many people have
All you're doing is spending a lot of money on death.

Adam Rixson (13)
William Edwards School

A Monster Under My Bed

There is a monster under my bed,
his eyes all big and red.
My covers up to my neck tight,
sometimes I sleep with a light.

9.30 is the time,
dragging my feet up the stairs with a sigh.
Pulling back the covers,
'Goodnight,' I say to my mother.

I get a tickle on my toe,
then a shiver on my nose.
Will he ever go away,
to myself 'I'm scared,' I say.

His big, pointy teeth,
waiting for me.
Will he disappear,
no, he'll always be near.

Today I can't see his pointy teeth,
what a relief.

My light goes off,
my quilt so soft.
Dreaming away,
he has gone away.

Katie West (12)
William Edwards School

THE CUP MATCH

I love rugby
I know I do
I play scrum half
So should you

We pack up for the scrum
The push of fate
Oh, the flanker
He arrives late

We start the scrum
In goes the ball
We hook it back
We win 'em all

Out to the fly half
He lost the ball
It's OK
We won it back in the maul

I pass it out
Along the line
We score a try
It was over in due time

The outside centre
Takes the kick
It goes over
'Cor that was quick!'

7-0 up
The whistle blew
We won the game
We go through.

William Plom (12)
William Edwards School